WOLVERINE TRACKS

DAG O. HESSEN

Translated by **LUCY MOFFATT**

Wolverine Tracks

ON THE TRAIL OF
MEMORY AND MEANING
IN THE WILD

GREYSTONE BOOKS
Vancouver/Berkeley/London

First published in English by Greystone Books in 2025
Originally published in Norwegian as *Jervesporet: Jakten på dyret, meningen og minnene i en krympende natur,*

25 26 27 28 29 5 4 3 2 1

Greystone Books Ltd.
greystonebooks.com

Cataloguing data available from Library and Archives Canada
ISBN 978-1-77840-189-3 (cloth)
ISBN 978-1-77840-190-9 (epub)

Editing for English edition by Paula Ayer
Proofreading by Alison Strobel
Jacket and text design by Fiona Siu
Jacket illustration by filo/iStock.com

Printed and bound in Canada on FSC® certified paper at Friesens. The FSC® label means that materials used for the product have been responsibly sourced.

Greystone Books thanks the Canada Council for the Arts, the British Columbia Arts Council, the Province of British Columbia through the Book Publishing Tax Credit, and the Government of Canada for supporting our publishing activities.

EU Safety Information: Easy Access System Europe, Mustamäe tee 50, 10621 Tallinn, Estonia, gpsr.requests@easproject.com.

This translation has been published with the financial support of NORLA.

Greystone Books gratefully acknowledges the xʷməθkʷəy̓əm (Musqueam), Sḵwx̱wú7mesh (Squamish), and səlilwətaɬ (Tsleil-Waututh) peoples on whose land our Vancouver head office is located.

Contents

ABOVE US THE SKY is white, beneath us lies the snow, and these two versions of white meet at the horizon. The sun, which has begun to make its presence felt after winter, is barely discernible as a diffuse glow behind the light cloud cover. All that interrupts the whiteness up here are small clusters of stunted downy birches. Farther down lies a birch forest and far below that a spruce-clad valley, beyond which, in the northwest, a row of peaks lines the horizon like wolverines' teeth. Dad and I are heading into the mountains. It's the winter vacation and we've skied from the cabin, through the forest, and beyond all the ski tracks, as so often before. In a dip where there's a willow thicket, ptarmigans have embroidered the snow with their intricate patterns, which are broken up by hare tracks. The ptarmigans slept in snow hollows here, part buried, part covered by the previous night's light snow, before shaking off the snowflakes at dawn, grazing on a breakfast of winter buds, and leaving only wing prints in the light, fresh snow by way of farewell. The tracks tell a silent tale of who has passed this way. Once in a while, the snow may be stained with blood, and you can read the drama that played out like red writing on a blank sheet of paper; but for the most part, the winter mountains are still and soundless. For the most part, they are simply white.

Suddenly, to our surprise, we encounter a track unlike all the others we usually see up here: the print of broad paws. It runs in a straight line from the horizon in the north and vanishes over the gentle mountain ridge to the east.

"Bear," I say.

"Wolverine," says Dad, who knows pretty much everything and is a veterinary surgeon besides.

Norway's biggest mustelid, he explains; a relative of the snow weasel and the stoat, with the appearance of a little bear. An animal hardly anyone gets to see. A compact bundle of wildness and strength almost without compare. It is undaunted by precipitous gorges, lynxes, wolves, or bears, and can dispatch a reindeer many times heavier than itself before biting off the head and hanging it high up in a tree—like a trophy. Its bite strength allows it to tackle frozen meat with ease and to crush even the most powerful thigh bones, and it is a perpetual motion machine that can walk forever. In short, the wolverine is a creature beyond measure, says Dad—a sober-minded man not given to dramatic exaggeration.

I stand there, elated, gazing at the fresh tracks. I place the basket of my ski pole alongside them and make a mental note of their rough size. The entire print seems to match Dad's description, evoking a beast of purposeful confidence, striding self-assuredly from one eternity to the next. The snow fell lightly last night but there is none in the tracks, which must mean that somewhere not so far ahead, it walks. The fabled beast. "Let's follow it," I beg

Dad, who nods his assent. So we turn southeast, following in the wolverine's footprints. We ski for maybe half an hour. The animal we are hunting seems to know exactly where it's going, but its route eventually takes it down a sheer birch-clad mountainside where the snow lies deep. For the wolverine, with its snowshoe-like paws, this is scarcely a challenge, but for us it'll be a dangerous struggle in the loose snow through dense birch forest. Dad calls a retreat. "We need to go back anyway," he reminds me as I stand there gazing after the trail with a wolverine at the other end. Perhaps we are closer than we guess, perhaps it's right behind the forest. Oh, to see a wild wolverine!

In the days that follow, I can't get this animal out of my head; and on our return from winter vacation I sacrifice a virgin notebook, neatly inscribing *Zoo Journal and Observations* on its cover. On the first page, I write a note in cursive hand:

> Wolverine. 1972. February 28. Saw wolverine tracks on the way from Øksendal to Friisbua (halfway). They crossed the ski tracks and were so big I could fit my whole palm in them. Length 6.5–7 inches, width 3.5–4 inches. Relatively fresh. Cool.

Now I stand here again, perhaps in precisely the same spot where the wolverine tracks crossed our path that day. Fifty years have passed. A lifetime. Dad is gone, but two new generations have arrived. There are no wolverine tracks here today, but I have accumulated half a century of determination and have decided to dedicate however much time it takes to following any tracks I come across.

Perhaps I'll find another wolverine trail, perhaps I'll see the fabled beast at last. If nothing else, perhaps I may find some remnants of lost youth, lived life, that intensity of feeling for nature I recall from my teenage years. Or is that the sole preserve of youth? Perhaps the feeling of springtime nature will do it—the vital spark, the lust for life, estrus mingled with warmth and spring sunshine and the surge of nature. But I'm also on the trail of the fascination that swept over me with such inexplicable force as I stood by the wolverine tracks with Dad and pictured this embodiment of condensed wildness. A feeling that was linked to the wolverine as primal power, wilderness in animal form, everything that is lost to us in a nature that is being steadily reduced to a tame vestige of its former self. The chances of seeing a wolverine are slim, vanishingly slim, and since I'm a different person now than fifty years ago, there is also little chance that I will revive the intense emotions from that phase of life when everything is opening up, our appetite for life is at its peak, and our senses are sharp and alive to impressions. Back then, no doors were closed, nothing had yet become routine, and most things in life were still new and unexperienced. For this reason, I have another, less ambitious goal as well. Quite simply to savor the feeling of being alive, of having time on my hands, of just being in nature, gliding into the wolverine's world. I have dreamed of that for fifty years too, but never made time for it.

Winter

ONCE ABOVE THE BIRCH LINE I turn due east, in the direction the wolverine tracks took back then. There's been a steady wind all winter and little snowfall. The snow underfoot is hard-packed, so it's easy going on backcountry skis; I float on top of it, just like a wolverine. Here are the last outposts of the mountain forest: a cluster of crooked downy birches that have managed to eke out an existence on the southern slope of Jammerdalshøgda—"Vale of Tears Mountain"—somewhat sheltered from the eternal north wind and with maximum exposure to sunlight. There are two sets of tracks by the birches, both raised—a phenomenon you sometimes see when the wind has been blowing for a while. The prints were made on a mild day when the snow was packed hard enough that the tracks remained, like a raised relief, after the wind had blasted away the uppermost layers of snow around them, like a hard granite formation in a landscape of easily weathered, soft limestone. One set of tracks was left by a ptarmigan, the other by a larger animal that *may* have been a wolverine. I ski up from a dip between two elevations; across the gentle slope rising to the south runs a constant river of restless snowflakes, driven by the wind, seeking a place of rest. The sun shines palely through the blanketing clouds, coaxing a silvery shimmer from the dancing, ever-shifting snow.

This is benign and easily traversed terrain. Over tens of millennia, the ice sent its arms out from Rondane, the high peaks to the north, wearing down all resistance along the way and leaving sand, gravel, and soil behind in the valleys. What remains is a tamed landscape of rounded peaks and valleys, in which only the central massif on this plateau has retained its wildness and grandeur. Low precipitation and a fairly unforgiving geology provide a foothold for only the most meager vegetation. But this barrenness is also what gives the landscape its charm—and light. The plateaus are carpeted white with snow in winter and lichen in summer. And millennia ago, roiling glacial rivers carved out valleys and ravines between the peaks, depositing soil in other places to create green oases of lushness.

At the highest point of the stretch between the peaks of Jammerdal, a plateau surrounded by mountains reveals itself to the southwest. It opens out into a birch forest and endless bogland south of the remote summer farm called Breistølen. This is a simple kind of farm known as a *seter*, which is not a permanent settlement but a place where farmers down in the valley bring their cattle and sheep for grazing in summertime. Two gaps in the low clouds let in a little light, which sweeps like slow, dimmed spotlights over all the white. Due south of where I am, I spy two black dots. That's where I'm headed. During my descent, there is nothing to indicate how steep it is in all this whiteness, but I'm familiar with the terrain and know that the slope here is smooth and safe. At one point, I pass a spot scattered with ripped-up lichen and black droplets of reindeer dung: a good sign for anyone on the track of wolverines, since *they* will be looking for reindeer; but this is the track of a solitary animal. Where is the herd?

The two black patches on the horizon expand to form the outline of a cabin and an outhouse. I have been to this cabin, Kluftbua, many times, but not for years now. This little cabin is the hub of my wolverine-tracking efforts, both geographically and in another sense. It is generously left open so anyone who is out and about in the mountains can use it.

Once there, I take off my skis and leave them on the lee side of the cabin, brush off the snow, and go inside. It's a log cabin with weather-beaten brown-stained cladding, framed by red bargeboards, with four solid beams and a ridgepole built to cope with any snowfall that may come. The cabin is neat and tidy—the people who pass through are clearly worthy of the confidence extended to them. Apart from a small hallway, which also serves as a woodstore, the cabin consists of a single room, with a wood-burning stove, a table with benches and stools, two candles, and bunk beds with sheepskins. What more could you want? Above the small-paned window hangs a picture of farmhands at work in front of a red cottage and barn. Two women turn the hay and place it in haystacks—this was before the days of hay-drying racks—and in the background is a man with a horse and cart. Apart from the bunk beds, the cabin is exactly the same as it was fifty years ago. I've sometimes spent the night here, and will do so again, but this is just a daytime visit. I sit down at the table and look through the small-paned window, peering up the slope that I will soon be tackling as I think about my late colleague, the biologist and author E. O. Wilson: "I have never seen a wild wolverine," he writes in his book *The Creation*, published in 2006—not a book about creation in the biblical sense, but a deeply felt homage to the marvelous diversity of life produced by evolution. The book is subtitled *An Appeal to Save Life on Earth* and is also aimed at those who view our planet as a work of creation. Wilson, the rational evolutionary biologist, says:

> No words and no art can capture the full depth and intricacy of the living world—as biologists have come increasingly to understand it. If a miracle is a phenomenon we cannot understand, then all species are something of a miracle. Each and every kind of organism, by virtue of the exacting conditions that produced it, is profoundly unique and shows its diagnostic traits reluctantly.

To elaborate on this, Wilson turns to the wolverine, one of the two animal species that particularly fascinated him (the other being ants, the group of animals he devoted most of his life to studying). He continues:

> This weasel-like mammal of the north woods is legendary for its ferocity, cunning, and elusiveness. Chunky in form, three to four feet long and weighing twenty to

> forty pounds, it is one of Earth's smallest top-tier predators. It feeds on everything from rats to deer. It can chase cougars and wolf packs away from downed prey and drag carcasses three times its own weight. It has fuzzy thick black fur, but this is no animal you'd want to pet. It has sharp teeth, a predator's retractable claws, and the face of a miniature bear... Individuals are both solitary and exceptionally shy of humans. They wander far and wide—here today, over there somewhere tomorrow, and gone for good the day after that.[1]

Fifty years on from my first visit here, I sit in Kluftbua once more, eating my packed lunch and watching the light shift as the clouds sail overhead. Impatient, I finish up quickly, put on my skis, and carry on gently upward and southward. Some way up the hillside, I look back at the cabin in all its isolation. Far off on the horizon, the white plateau meets a restless sky in constantly shifting shades of gray. It grows more overcast and once more the snow sweeps over the mountainsides, but I continue to advance until everything around me is perfectly white. It's a lovely feeling, this, to stand here enshrouded in white nothingness, no points of reference in the landscape except when I look down and see Fridtjof Nansen, polar explorer, scientist, and humanist: his portrait on my skis. The last hero whose glory is still unfaded.

In this white no-man's-land, surrounded only by the soft soughing of the wind and the whisper of snow crystals, I simply *am*. I'm not due anywhere. Why have I done so little of what, as a youth, I expected to be a central part of my life? Although I constantly walk, or mostly run, *out* in nature, I am much more rarely *in* nature. I've done plenty of cross-country skiing, but at constantly increasing speeds, on increasingly well-groomed tracks. For many years now, I've barely strayed outside the tracks, with the exception of a few summit hikes in spring, but even then it's been a matter of straight up and straight back down again, my eye constantly on the clock. There's always something that needs to be done, and my outdoor excursions have simply been a hasty means of relieving pressure in between duties and obligations, dictated by time. There's always been this drive to do *something useful*, to justify my own existence, given that I was lucky enough to be born in the best place in the world during the best era in the world. Perhaps my primary drive hasn't been duty but rather a quest for meaning, or at least for a *feeling* of meaning, and an acknowledgment that it can only be achieved by making a positive contribution to something greater than oneself, something more enduring, something right, something others can benefit from. I'm referring here to meaning *in* one's own life—the meaning *of* life is something quite different. And the more you get done, the more meaning is created. Indeed one variant of the hedonist's goal of achieving the greatest possible happiness is to be of the greatest possible use; but since, to a certain extent, usefulness can be converted into happiness by doing or achieving something, hedonism and the ethics of duty are related.

When I truly discovered nature as a young man, I thought I would spend my life out here, or at least a great deal of it. In the forests and mountains. Gradually and imperceptibly, busyness sneaked into my life; one thing led to another. My existence was constantly made more efficient: faster computers, faster roads, faster everything. More standardization and time-saving routines. But the more efficient I became, the more of a hurry I was in and the less time I had. A five-minute wait at the bus stop became an eternity that was impossible to bear without my cell phone as a diversion. A ten-second wait in front of a slow PC has become irritating dead time. And all the while, the river of life runs mercilessly faster. Out here in the mountains, time is different. I can stand here and simply be. It's a sanctuary of slowness and analog time.

My father, who was from a small mountainside farm on an island in Western Norway, was a duty ethicist and a true-born son of the region's Calvinistic culture of thrift. But he was also a man possessed of great calm, life wisdom, and an extensive poetry collection. As I stand enveloped in the white and feel the enormous contrast between the timelessness here and my daily treadmill, I find myself thinking of "The Busy Man," a poem my father knew by heart. I recall some verses and see just how well Jan-Magnus Bruheim captured it:

> He has so much ground to cover.
> It's vital to travel fast.
> There was much for him to do
> Each day brought more tasks than the last.
>
> The end of the day is approaching
> He stands bent over his stick
> And asks: What has life given to me
> How did it go by so quick?

Thus he hurried his way through life
Without ever getting a grip
A joy ran behind him on the road
But never caught up with him.

But that isn't quite accurate either, because there's undoubtedly pleasure to be had from doing things, being useful, trying to find out what we're good for; and, on a good day, from savoring the joy of success too. Perhaps it may bring us peace in the long run, but neither meaning nor happiness are achieved by simply lying on our backs in the heather and watching the clouds drift by. And the very same Nansen who gazes up at me from my skis has retained his glory and luster precisely because he managed to achieve so very many great things, as a humanist, for starters. At the same time, his life was a constant tug-of-war between duties and pleasures—the former being science, lecture tours, diplomacy, travels, and teeming crowds, while hunting, nature, and simplicity were the central sources of happiness in his existence. Nonetheless, his life turned out to be dominated by duty, and his moments of solitude and silence beneath the open skies were probably all the more intensely enjoyable for being islands of pleasure in an ocean of its opposite. But the duty was also self-imposed; he betrays the secret motivation for his tremendous life's work in a letter to his sister, Ida: "Also, this fear that one's name will not outlive one's own body... this quest for a single basis for hope." It is the fear that everything is in vain. Death also provides a considerable stimulus for personal vanity. We cannot underestimate posterity as motivation—indeed, some people seem to conduct their lives with an eye to their future obituaries and eulogies, even though both tend to be larded with vacuous flattery these days. Being remembered as a good person and one who did something for others is the closest we get to achieving even an iota of immortality. And this doesn't just apply to saints or empire builders; anyone can feel this motivation. But the vast majority of us face the prosaic limitation that we actually have to earn a living. Yet here I stand in all this white and know that the cumulative contribution of my entire life is at best a ripple on the ocean—so why haven't I lived a slow life out in nature instead?

I don't know quite how long I stand here, sunk in my own thoughts; but in the end, the wind nips and the cold pierces my clothing. I had no greater goal that day than to see again the place where my father and I had found wolverine tracks, to revisit Kluftbua and, beyond that, just to experience absolute silence and absolute whiteness. If it had been a windless, clear day, I would have carried on for a while, perhaps well into the twilight, then switched on my headlamp to light my way back; but current weather conditions are hardly inviting. The day draws to a close as I ski down into the river valley that starts by Kluftbua, where the Breia River meanders down toward Gudbrandsdalen. This valley is a good place when it's windy: I've sought shelter here before after being surprised by bad weather. It's one of those lovely valleys that are easy to cross, where willows and small birch trees offer ideal grazing for ptarmigans and hares. The wind eases off and the sun comes out again. Down here, there are still plenty of animal tracks, and open holes in the ice where the river lives and bears witness to the imminence of spring. I follow it almost all the way down to the summer farm, Breistølen. Some years back, a bear was observed here, sitting out on the bogland for an hour, devouring a sheep. Not by me, sadly. I've never seen a bear in the wild on the Norwegian mainland.

I ski onward, up the birch-clad hillside, heading due west; it's steep and I sink deep into the snow. I consider putting skins on my skis, but short-term laziness wins the day. After climbing diagonally for half an hour, I reach a flatter stretch on the upper edge of the birch belt. Although it's outside their normal route, I once stumbled across a reindeer here one winter's day many years ago. Almost literally. I came to an abrupt halt by a large hole in the snow, from which tracks radiated in all directions: a few fox tracks, but mostly wolverine prints. And down there in the hole lay the reindeer, or what was left of it. Much of it had been eaten, and even the larger bones had been chewed over. Whether the animal had been killed or just found by the wolverine it was impossible to say—probably the latter. And what the reindeer was even doing here, likely far away from its flock, was another matter altogether. The wolverine may well have managed to pick up the scent, even that of a reindeer deep-frozen beneath the snow, possibly from as far away as Jammerdal. And then it had dug its way down, gashed open the frozen hide, gnawed through frost-stiffened flesh, and devoured the entrails. Afterward, perhaps, it lay on the outcrop up here, full to bursting, and gazed into the mountains, feeling, in its wolverine way, that life was good. It returned again at intervals of several days to eat the meat and then the marrow, enjoying times of plenty. But this was long ago. That wolverine no longer exists, and today there's no trace of anything here—not even a ptarmigan track across the peaks.

I ski down the other side, cross a boggy area, head up a hillside through the birch forest, and then I reach *my* place. I haven't spent the night here for many years, but the cabin is in good condition—my father saw to that.

The architecture and interior are what might be described as "typical 1970s," although it's actually from the 1960s, and was mostly built by my father and grandfather. A plaid sofa, plaid curtains, small-paned windows, pine furnishings, and paraffin lamps. A cabin that consists of one bedroom divided in two, a stove, and a corner sofa, and which is slightly better equipped than its predecessor—the one-room shack that wasn't originally a holiday cabin but a spartan overnight shelter for people with vital business out in the mountains: lumberjacks or shepherds. My cabin is a luxury in the sense that it was built for leisure and pleasure, albeit with the minimalism and thrift of the 1960s. It was a place to drive to in our VW during the winter and Easter vacations—hauling our baggage half a mile up to the cabin on pulk sleds, lighting the stove, digging out the well to collect water, and then waiting for the indoor temperature to become bearable. Which could take hours. It was a cabin built for slow time, where cards and board games were all the entertainment we needed. We had no idea what cabin life would look like in the 2020s—the constant battles over plug sockets for everyone's chargers, the continuous stream of digital interruptions and notifications of all kinds, or discussions about the choice of TV station, and who should have first dibs on which bathroom. Our simple cabin eventually acquired a gas oven, which made my mother happy. Then came solar panels, and no one missed the stink of paraffin lamps. When he was really old, my father also wired the cabin, providing enough electricity for a few lamps, a coffee percolator, and a couple of extra plug sockets. By then, the roads were also plowed in winter.

Eventually the Market itself took charge, altering Norwegian cabin life for good. Landowners sold once-worthless tracts of barren mountain terrain to professional construction companies at a time when purchasing power was on the rise. It wasn't just that there were more cabins, but also *bigger* cabins, with bathrooms and underfloor heating, saunas, washing machines, dishwashers, and brushed-steel fridges. Fifty years ago there were 170,000 cabins in Norway, with an average size of roughly 550 square feet. Now there are close to half a million, many of them holiday homes, complete with infrastructure, and an average area of roughly 1,000 square feet. And, as with most other things, the pace of development has accelerated. In this case, it has advanced so rapidly that the effects on highland nature are visible to us, although other changes occur so gradually, even from a fifty-year perspective, that we are able to get used to them: our frames of reference shift. The landscape as it used to be is erased from our memories, and we identify the changes only when we see old photos or statistics. But some cabins, like this one, are still cabins.

I put my backpack down beside the outer door and find the key. It's still hanging where it always has—not very well hidden, but there's not much worth stealing here anyway. Then I unlock the door, grab the broom that I know stands in the vestibule to the right of the door, where it always has done, brush the snow off my boots, go inside, and open the curtains. In the little bathroom hangs the cabin's only mirror. It's small and dusty but even in the poor light, I see that the decades have left their mark. It's still me staring back, the resemblance to my confirmation portrait remains, but there's a different cast to my face; I have more wrinkles, a shadow beneath the cheekbones that wasn't there before, and some gray along my temples, which will spread implacably. Most of 1972 me has been replaced, cell by cell, many times over, without any break in my history; everything has advanced with infinite slowness. Despite the constant renewal, aging has followed its course, and even my innermost me—the recipe itself, my DNA—is not precisely the same. Time has taken a toll on it too, and the repair systems have found it increasingly difficult to keep up with the eternal mutations; epigenetic changes cause the message to be read slightly differently, my cell walls are growing stiffer, wrinkles are emerging, everything is graying. While I see no positives to aging, the alternative is hardly preferable. Besides, aging is so wisely arranged that our vision deteriorates over time, making it more difficult for us to see our own decline. Yet the mirror still shows me much of the boy who stared back at me fifty years ago. Less expectant, but more clued up. Back then, I knew nothing about how my life would turn out. The only thing I knew was that I would grow older. Paradoxically, it bothered me much more then than now.

Life comes about through random events but within a given framework. The most important components of my cosmic winning ticket in life were, of course, a good childhood with good parents in the best country in the world during the best era in the world. The mere fact of being born is an utterly improbable event, and it is dizzying to realize that we are among the—for now—most recent links in an unbroken chain of life. And the years that have made up my own life: every single one of them, indeed every week, has contained unexpected events, good and bad. Mostly good, but also bad, very bad. Each of these milestones offers an opportunity to consider that the road might have been different.

Although I am demonstrably changed, the cabin is more or less the same. And luckily it is in a location that has not fallen victim to the urbanization of Norway's highlands and mountain pastures via holiday cabin developments; on the whole, the landscape is the way I recall it from my boyhood. The reassurance of recognition: something is unchanged in an accelerating world.

On the whole, emotions are rational. They are dictated by chemical signals and signaling pathways in the brain, many of which originated far back in our evolutionary prehistory. The more closely a mammal is related to us, the more of these signal substances—and emotions—we share. Some are fundamental: not just hunger, fear, aggression, and sex drive, but also the pleasure, joy, caring, and empathy triggered by our reward hormones. Longing is also rational to the extent that it provokes us to action, but nostalgia is a peculiar case: it's hard to say what purpose it serves, and it is probably more a mood than a primary emotion. Old cabins are nostalgia, which is why we cling to them and view them as essential components of our identity. Our parents are gone, families are scattered, the children have moved out, but at our cabins, everything is the same as ever. We associate them with happy holiday memories and a carefree childhood existence. But this also makes them a reminder of everything that is no more and will never return. For me: youth, future, a good father. My sister Marit.

I didn't become aware of death until I was eight, when a girl in my class suddenly died. Since our school was beside the cemetery, my class was taken along when the little coffin was lowered into the grave in the presence of the inconsolable parents. After this, the waterfall roar of death lay over the valley and I was often overwhelmed by fear at the thought that this wonderful life would one day irrevocably end; that I would no longer be able to experience springtime out in nature. I look at the tiny mementos left behind by Marit, which are still here in the cabin—painted vases, pieces of embroidery—and feel that death has lost its sting. Perhaps it's resignation or fatalism: we accept our fate, and that brings a kind of peace. Yet it is still difficult to reconcile myself to losing the opportunity to experience spring in the mountains forever.

When death broke in on a hitherto safe and predictable world, and my sense of meaning crumbled, nature and the mountains became my fixed points of reference. I still feel that way now, too, when faced again with the ancient mountains, with the familiar landscape, with what endures.

The cabin is, after all, an ephemeral construction in the grand scheme of things, just like me. Nostalgia is one thing, but at an old cabin, it can tip over into sentimentality—which is nostalgia on steroids: a dysfunctional longing that can only lead to despondency.

THE MICE HAVE been partying here and played havoc with the contents of one of the cupboards. But they were unlucky enough to end up in the wrong one, the one without any food. They have, however, chewed pretty much everything in there to bits: the candles, a few wine corks, bars of soap, and polystyrene. And they chewed holes in all the packets of washing detergent, so that the powder has trickled out and blended with enormous amounts of mouse droppings. The pots and pans are filthy. The other cupboard, containing packets of cookies, old chocolate, and other treats, is untouched. If only they'd known. At the very back of the cupboard I find some cookies marked "Best before 1995" that still taste perfectly fine. After sweeping up the mouse droppings, I dig out the well, fetch a couple of buckets of water, wash the floor, and boil the utensils I'll need for cooking. The cold has settled in the walls and after two hours of intensive stoking, the wood-burning stove has only pushed the indoor temperature up to precisely freezing point.

I eat, throw a few logs on the fire, and even manage to find a slug of cognac left over from Dad's day. Then I take a book out of my pack: *Wolverine,* by the Norwegian nature writer Mikkjel Fønhus. Between the end of the 1950s and his death in 1973, Fønhus published a new novel every year, and when I was a child, I would always get the latest one for Christmas. Early on Christmas Eve, I would sneak off and vanish into Fønhus's world. By Christmas Day, the book would be finished—the story often ending in death for both the animal and its nemesis, the hunter. The unusual thing about Fønhus was that his sympathies lay with the animal, but it was more than that, too: he saw the world through the prism of the animal's emotions. *Wolverine* was among the Fønhus books I didn't own, and it took some effort to track it down in a secondhand bookshop. In 1959, it had cost twenty kroner; now I happily paid three hundred. "In the depths of dusk that same evening," Fønhus writes, "an animal as big as a medium-sized dog came creeping out of a talus."

> He started to head east, walking on big, broad paws and somewhat bowed legs, following a path that was slightly crooked, yet steadily aiming for a broad, high peak deep in the mountains—Ørneflag... He roamed in the mountains in the manner typical of his kind: if he came to a fair-sized rock, he would jump up onto it, stand there looking around, and scent the air; this made it easier for him to detect whether there were any animals nearby that he could try and sneak up on... At midnight, he slid like a shadow across a ridge just below Ørneflag—his form visible against the starlight-sprinkled vault of the heavens.[2]

The wolverine hunter, Heine Juvet, isn't a bad man; he too must scratch out a livelihood on his barren mountain farm, and the bounty on wolverines helps him make ends meet. Besides, the wolverine has been helping itself to Heine's cattle. Heine isn't burdened by any deep ecological notions about the wolverine's capacity for suffering, and this is a war whose ends justify all means—including poison and wolverine traps. Fønhus expresses the point through the words of a local reindeer herder: "These animals were placed in the mountains by the Devil and not Our Lord!"[3] Eventually, the animal is caught in the snare. "The wolverine lay there with the trap upended before him; his paw protruded from between the clamped steel jaws, and he lay there gazing at this paw, which prevented him from freeing his leg, escaping from this bind..."[4] In the end, the wolverine gnaws off the lifeless paw and becomes known as Threefeet.

I put a big birch root on the fire and go over to the outhouse to fetch more wood. From the outer door, it's about ten steps through the snow. In just a couple of hours, February will be over, but the darkness is in full command. It's a cold winter night, there's not a light to be seen, and twinkling stars are everywhere. When was the last time I saw such a starry sky? I'd forgotten how overwhelming it is. To the left of the door is the privy, concealed by a curtain, and on the floor stand paint cans whose bottoms are coated with dried wood stain; there are tools and saws, a chopping block and axe, some folding chairs leaned up against the walls, and two rows of firewood that line the transverse wall from floor to ceiling. Dad was a man of impeccable order, but also a hoarder. No one who grew up on a smallholding on the west coast of Norway during the hardscrabble 1930s has ever thrown anything out, and Dad had his own way of straightening out crooked nails and bashing the bristles of old paintbrushes until they were soft. He was thrifty but never mean. He has left me a substantial legacy of firewood here in the outhouse, while more is stacked outside along the cabin's lee wall—and it's had many years to dry out. Mouse droppings are scattered everywhere here, the floor is covered in them. The mice have gnawed away at tarbrushes and leather straps, but that's meager fare even for them.

I find the broom and sweep out the worst of it before going into the cabin and fetching a lump of cheese that I nail down close to the outer door. A couple of feet away, I set down a candle. Then I put on a woolly hat and a warm sheepskin coat and sit down on the polystyrene seat of the privy. That insulating polystyrene was the true herald of a new era at the cabin. It is absolutely silent for ten minutes. I've decided to give the mice twenty minutes before going back inside to the warmth of the wood-burning stove. Then there's a rustling inside the woodpile, followed by more rustling, and a solitary mouse creeps over to the cheese, planning to snatch it to safety; but, as I said, the cheese is nailed down. Hunger and fear battle in the tiny creature, but hunger wins out. And in that same instant, I see a small triangular head through a crack in the door—a snow weasel, which hurls itself at the mouse. A feeble shriek, a brief struggle, and the weasel scurries out, effortlessly carrying the mouse in its jaws although the body probably weighs almost as much as its own. It all happens so fast that I barely have time to register the drama before it's over. I'm left perplexed after the brief but intense scene. I had no intention of contributing to the mouse's death, but now that I think about it, I do recall seeing weasel tracks leading to a hole in the snow outside. It strikes me there's a certain irony in the fact that, on my quest to find the wolverine, I've met its smallest relative instead. Second cousin to the pine marten and smaller cousin to the stoat, it's among the world's smallest predators and a dangerous little devil for mice, even though it usually weighs well below a hundred grams. A mustelid with the compressed strength and wildness of the wolverine, scaled down to half a percent of the size of its larger relative. Incidentally, a pine marten once came down the chimney of the cabin and exited via the stove. It had the place to itself and after sweeping its way down through the flue, it inspected all the beds, scattering unfeasible amounts of soot over them before abandoning its search for food and leaving the same way it had come.

Back in front of the stove with Fønhus: Heine has been tracking Threefeet for hours. The wolverine now leaves a characteristic trail behind it: three paw marks and a fourth, lighter print. Toward evening, the track leads Heine to a rough talus. After fashioning a rudimentary torch, Heine creeps in after the wolverine, shotgun at the ready. He manages to fire one shot inside before the torch goes out, and after a tremendous struggle in the darkness, he catches the wolverine. But outside, above the talus, tracks appear: three paw prints, and a lighter impression from the fourth. Threefeet is not the animal a badly scratched Heine skins some hours later.

> The tip of the knife blade cut and cut carefully beneath the skin and as it came loose from the body, he saw how it veritably bulged with muscles, making it clear

> why this far from large animal was capable of the feats it sometimes achieved; Heine once saw a wolverine drag away an entire reindeer buck after killing it.[5]

A friend of mine also witnessed just such an episode. During a winter hunt in the north, he noticed a reindeer grazing on the very edge of a wind-blasted ledge on the other side of the valley. He took out his binoculars and saw a compact black hunter sneaking upward, concealed by an outcrop—immediately beneath the deer yet outside its field of vision. It climbed all the way up and then, in one explosive movement, leaped over the edge and clamped its jaws on the reindeer's throat. The struggle didn't last long. This was an upgraded version of the weasel's lightning-fast and fatal attack on the mouse.

There is an almost endless supply of literature about people in nature and nature in people. I've read my share of it and much of it revolves around this familiar theme: Life is simplest, best, and most authentic in the great outdoors. Some of the writing is mawkish and naive, but almost all of it conveys something that is hard to articulate: the way nature enriches us, both through what it is and what it is *not*. Many writers side with the animals against us humans, the attackers, and some point out the similarities between concentration camps and modern livestock farms. Others seek to understand us humans against the backdrop of "the others"—animals, that is—interpreting humankind through the prism of the animalistic, while others again take the opposite approach, writing anthropomorphic literature that seeks to understand animals using us humans as a starting point. This is the approach Fønhus takes, without seeming naive or phony. And no one ever learns what the wolverine thinks, although it clearly has its own views about hunting, the need to hide away from people, and the incomprehensible iron jaws of the animal trap. Ever since Darwin established the interrelatedness of all life, our ability to describe reality through the animal's senses—to the extent that this is even possible—has undergone a continual process of maturation. It makes a pleasant change from writing that expresses hatred of predators, a legacy of the days when they were strong and we were weak. Now the situation is reversed, yet the hatred smolders on.

Perhaps it has something to do with the fact that we humans are animals too. We have an almost horrified fascination with the bestial, perhaps especially within ourselves—an aspect we see as the antithesis of the ongoing self-domestication that has been a central component of our species' project of becoming human. From biology to philosophy, high literature to crime fiction, we see the appeal of the bestial everywhere: savagery, desire, bloodthirstiness, the dark, and the dangerous. Therein lies the appeal of the wolverine, too, and of the myths of its savagery and bloodthirsty nature. Admittedly no species can compete with the wolf when it comes to mythologization and scrutiny, but it has now become so thoroughly monitored, described, and managed that it has lost some of the mystique that the wolverine still possesses. I have, by the way, never met a wolf out in nature, although I would dearly love to have that experience.

Part of my plan for this trip is to savor the lovely slowness and the pictures that my imagination creates when I read; but right now, I've restricted my selection of fireside reading to literature about the wolverine. There's not that much of it. I skim-read Ida Fjeldbraaten's novel *Wolverine.* She too is on the trail of the animal's wildness, as it relates to our own latent wildness. The book is described as "a tender, urgent tale of bodily fluids, jaws, teeth, mud, and bites, about nature and culture." I appreciate the author's attempt to see the wildness through the wolverine's eyes and her exploration of the borderland between nature and culture, which we speak and think of as two separate spheres of life, even though they are actually closely interwoven. We are more creatures of nature than we tend to think; most of our drives, pleasures, and pains are embedded in our lives, in our emotions, and choices, admittedly often transformed into and camouflaged as culture. Animals have culture too, even if it doesn't manifest itself in the form of churches, music, or literature.

I also leaf through Jon Michelet's book of the same title, *Wolverine.* It may not be his most readable novel, but it is, perhaps, the most curious or burlesque. While the early pages give no clear indication of whether the wolverine in the book is real or metaphorical, Michelet has dug up some priceless quotations that hint at the origin of the wolverine's reputation as a glutton, as well as its mythology. First up is Peder Claussøn Friis, who claimed in 1599 that the wolverine was such a glutton that it would eat a horse in short order, press itself between two trees to squeeze itself empty, and then start eating again. What's more, the people of Setesdal, in southern Norway, said that it could eat an entire reindeer, both meat and bones, in a single night; their hunters added that it had eaten a whole horse in the same time.[6] In addition, Michelet has tracked down the work of a certain Professor Rasch, probably the zoologist and naturalist Halvor Heyerdahl Rasch, who claimed, 150 years after Claussøn Friis, that the wolverine "could cause no small damage, in certain places, especially in the kingdom's northern landscapes, and especially to the reindeer and the winter provisions of the Laplanders"—a complaint that could just as easily have been written today. People were as keen on imitation then as they are now, and the myth of the wolverine has obviously grown with every retelling. Claussøn Friis's source was a 1555 book written by Olaus Magnus of Sweden, elegantly entitled *Historia de gentibus septentrionalibus*—a splendid overview of the Nordic peoples and their lives that also deals with significant animals. Olaus Magnus, too, describes the wolverine's greed but contents himself with the claim that it can eat until its belly is as tight as a drum. Claussøn Friis added the detail about the horse. The peculiar assertion that it squeezes between two trees to empty its gut so that it can continue its feast is, however, identical in both sources. The wolverine is known as the "glutton" in the United States, and its Latin name has the same meaning, repeated—*Gulo gulo*—as if to underscore just what a big eater it is.

The wolverine's mythology goes far back in time. The cryptic inscription on a famous runestone, which was found in southern Norway and dates back to between 200 and 500 BCE, indicates that this is a memorial stone to a "guest" and ends with the runes "ek erafar," which is interpreted as "I, the wolverine." That may be a nickname the rune carver gave himself, alluding to the wolverine's fearlessness and strength, but he may also have worn a cloak of wolverine fur, assumed an animal's guise. The wolverine was considered to be the dog of a race of fairy folk: a *hulder*'s hound. Olaus Magnus writes a great deal about the wolverine, sometimes stating obvious facts—its flesh is not good to eat—and other times speaking about magical aspects of the animal, such as the power its claws and teeth have over everything from physical ailments to spirits. Wolverine blood with honey was served at weddings, and wolverine fat had curative properties. First and foremost, though, Olaus Magnus praises the marvelous quality of its pelt: it is one of the most prized furs and is worn by princes and nobles. What's more, he adds, wolverine fur has this magical property: anyone who sleeps beneath it dreams of the wolverine—or more precisely dreams *as* a wolverine.

THE FIRST NIGHT in the cabin I sleep better than I have for years: nine hours of deep, dreamless slumber. I don't even dream about the wolverine, but then again, I'm not lying under a wolverine pelt, am I? When I awake, I discover that it has snowed in the night, but the morning sun breaks through the ever-lighter sprinkling of snow. This is a day I have been looking forward to intensely: hours outdoors without a watch, a cell phone, or any particularly concrete plans. It is March 1 and the days are now light enough for ski trips lasting late into the evening. I take my time lighting the stove but eat breakfast standing up as I make myself a proper packed lunch. From the cabin, I ski through the birch forest and cross the bog again. This time, I cross a low forest-clad hill on its southern flank. No animals have yet dared venture out after the night's snowfall. Any creature that leaves tracks immediately after it has snowed alerts potential hunters to the fact that the animal at the end of the trail can't be far off.

But right on the other side of the gentle ridge a drama has recently played out. It started in a hollow beneath a dense juniper bush, where a hare leaped up in panic and headed off on a wild zigzag dash. From the other side of the juniper, a fox had come sauntering along, probably quite oblivious to the hare. Its tracks give no sign that it was sneaking up on prey—only of an acceleration when the hare revealed itself, shooting out like a projectile right under the fox's nose. A wild chase back and forth ensued, and I can't tell whether the tangle of tracks leads anyplace, but since there's neither blood nor any sign of a fight, it seems likely that the hare escaped scared but unscathed—yet again. As we know, the hare runs for its life, while the fox runs after food. It is surprisingly uncommon to find dead animals in the wild, other than by the roadside, which probably means that they get eaten. A couple of times, I've found a dead moose or reindeer, and once a dead fox too. A beautiful specimen with a thick winter pelt lay dead on the snow one sunny day in March—out in the middle of the mountains without any signs of wound or injury. The raven hadn't yet arrived. I got my father, a veterinarian, to do an autopsy (the cause of death was, prosaically, a twisted colon), and after it was skinned, I got a hundred and fifty kroner for the fur, or was it a hundred?

It was poor compensation for both my work and that beautiful pelt, at any rate.

The snow-covered track up to the summer farm winds its way onward through the birch forest, ending at one of my favorite spots out here. A sunny birch-covered hillside where the Breia River runs past on its way from Inner Breitjønn tarn by way of a long river valley down in the birch forest, before starting its long and meandering descent to the main river, Lågen, down in Gudbrandsdalen. The river runs in little rapids here, causing the open water to glitter in the sun. In the calmer stretches, snow bridges have formed. There are always plenty of tracks here: hares and foxes, of course, as well as ptarmigans, weasels, and often moose. But not today, not so soon after a snowfall. I've often noticed how there tend to be plenty of animal tracks in precisely the kind of terrain that instantly lifts my spirits. Maybe it's not so surprising. Sunny, south-facing slopes with broad vistas and water in the vicinity are vital for humans and animals alike. The feeling of well-being comes from the brain's dose of reward hormones that tell us: this is good, seek this out. In the case of us humans, the hormonal effect is often enhanced by a layer of good (or bad) memories, or the nostalgic joy of the familiar revisited. On this birch-covered hillside, both factors come into play for me.

I test the largest snow bridge with my ski pole before crossing the river and gliding over the pastureland of Breistølen, the summer farm that stands here like a royal mansion, utterly isolated against the backdrop of the mountains. On the other side of the pastureland, I set off into the open birch forest with the bare mountain behind it. Sun on snow on mountain. The most beautiful sight I know. The snow is so powdery I sink down into the juniper bushes beneath, so I head for more open areas where the wind has packed the snow more tightly. But look there! A purposeful track runs through the fresh snow: a predator at the top of the food chain with no reason to fear that others may discover its trail. It has a long stride length, but when I reach the tracks, I see that they don't have the typical three-by-three pattern; nor are the paw prints those of a wolverine. It must have been a big fox—an uncommonly big fox, admittedly, but still not the animal I'm here to find. Yet it has walked here with the self-assurance of a wolverine, rather than scurrying among the bushes and brushwood in search of mice and voles as foxes more typically do. Perhaps it knows of some carrion somewhere out here in the mountains. This year, life is a bit easier for animals like the fox because the light snowfall enables them to dig out lemmings or various species of voles; once in a blue moon, they may feast on a ptarmigan, a hare, or a dead moose or reindeer, but beyond that, it's almost impossible to grasp how they manage to survive the winter out here in the mountains.

On the upper edge of the forest, I follow the flank of the mountain ridge southward, then, maintaining the same altitude, I turn east. All the way, I savor the freedom and pleasure that are only afforded us in brief bursts over the course of our lives. It's still morning with a hint of spring; the sun warms me, and the day and the open mountain lie ahead. Nothing is pressing. No one is waiting. As I head east, the birch forest below passes out of sight and everything is framed in white, but visibility is good even though the wind is picking up today as well. There are no signs of ptarmigan tracks anywhere, not until I reach the innermost part of a dip in the landscape, the depression south of Øverlihøgda where the willow thicket ekes out an existence. Here, a little flock of the birds has embroidered the surrounding terrain, crisscrossing through the undergrowth. They were here recently, but are now gone.

My only goal today is to roam in the mountains in the hope of spotting reindeer or wolverines—or, more realistically, wolverine tracks. It's not unusual to see reindeer here at this time of year incidentally: they tend to wander across the wind-scoured heights where it's easy to find food to graze on beneath the thin layer of snow. And reindeer numbers have actually risen sharply since the days when they, too, were hunted to critically low levels. Despite my aimlessness, I've decided to make three stops. The first reveals itself as a dark formation amid all the white when I breast the hill and gaze across to where the terrain starts to slope down toward a remote and desolate valley, Imsdalen. As I come closer, the contours of an enormous metal skeleton come into view: the remains of a German Junkers Ju 52, which crash-landed here on Friday, October 30, 1942. The plane had taken off from the airport near Oslo at 8:30 that morning and was bound for the far north of Norway. Stops were scheduled along the way to the north, but the flight never made it that far. It met strong gales and a dense, sleety snowstorm over the Ringebu Mountains. Ice on the wings and poor visibility forced the plane down here. The captain died in the crash landing and another crew member was badly injured. Four men set off down to the village to fetch help, while two stayed behind to help the injured man. The four succeeded in finding their exhausted way to human habitation but were incapable of explaining the location of the plane wreck. Not until November 3 did the bad weather lift, allowing searchers to find the wreck. The crew members who had stayed behind were safe and sound, and the wounded German was seated inside the plane with his pistol drawn, possibly ready to take his own life. All three men were rescued, but the wounded man died soon afterward.

1942 seems like ancient history now—almost as distant as the Napoleonic Wars. Yet it was a mere thirty years prior to the day that Dad and I stood by the wolverine tracks in 1972, which, in turn, was fifty years prior to this moment in which I stand here, in the sunshine and snowdrifts that so beautifully drape the plane's cockpit and fuselage, amid the endless, peaceful white. In 1942, Dad was young, only slightly older than I was in 1972. The world in which he came to adulthood—from the war's end to 1972—was brimming with optimism. Progress was being made, life was becoming easier; Norwegians got cars, TVs, bigger houses, eventually holiday homes, and ever more commodities, and we saw no reason we shouldn't have even more. From the green branch of a tree that appeared to be growing into a cloudless sky, the world—at least as seen from Norway—seemed filled with boundless promise. Fifty years ago, the Norwegian prime minister was Trygve Bratteli, who had returned emaciated from German captivity after the war ended. He was born into a reality recorded in black and white, in which men came home from work in coats and hats while mothers were homemakers. I recall Bratteli as an extremely serious man, which is scarcely surprising after all those years in prison; but his gravity also reflected an age in which life was fundamentally serious, most had experienced scarcity, and public irony was an alien concept to all but a few. We young people didn't feel that we had an invisible safety net.

In 1972 came the decisive switch from black and white to color. The monochrome photographs of the 1960s depicting Dad in a hat and Grandfather with a pipe gave way to color photos, now bleached and faded, in which both hat and pipe are absent. Yet the people still look curiously dated, with their old-fashioned hairstyles and brown-checked clothes, often posing in front of strange, square-bodied cars. Nowadays the 1970s look like an exercise in bad taste; we rarely say "typical seventies style" in admiring tones. The first color TV broadcasts were piloted that year. Norway held a referendum on membership in the EU—or the European Economic Community, as it was then known. "No to the EEC and price rises!" chanted those of us back then who were already engaged in an incipient protest against both the omnipotence of capital and the sudden sense that the big wide world was encroaching on us and wanted to take charge.

1972 was a turning point in our history when we (or some of us at least) began to feel that we could no longer assume tomorrow would be an even better day; that the consumer snowball we had set rolling had now grown so enormous that it determined its own speed. While it is true that the great acceleration had already taken off in around 1960 and can even be traced back to the industrial revolution, growth in those days was still a means to a better life—not an end in itself or a necessity if we were to feed a seemingly insatiable system. The growth in the human population and human impact had already shifted into high gear, even though there were still "only" 3.8 billion of us on the planet. It had taken 300,000 years for us to become so numerous. And then we spent the next fifty years reaching 8 billion—more than doubling our number in this gamma-ray burst of time. In 1972, the concentration of CO_2 in the atmosphere was 327 ppm; but by then it was already ten years since Charles David Keeling—originator of the world's longest continuous record of CO_2 measurements, using data collected in Hawaii—had demonstrated a significant rise in CO_2 levels. And this increase was primarily due to our fossil-fuel consumption, which would, Keeling asserted sixty years ago, heat up the planet if the rise continued. Now CO_2 levels have exceeded 420 ppm and will continue to climb for a long time to come. Incidentally, Rachel Carson published *Silent Spring* at the same time as Keeling issued his first warning. Her revelation that nature was not impervious to our emissions triggered the world's first green wave.

Although we still felt back in 1972 that there were few of us humans amid an infinite nature, that the sky and the sea were still blue and endless; and although we took it as read that prosperity would continue to grow for the foreseeable future, the first clouds had appeared on the horizon. In 1972, a group of scientists known as the Club of Rome published *The Limits to Growth*, which would sell fifty million copies and prompt an intense ideological debate about this issue. The flip side of prosperity manifested itself in various ways and, for the first time, the concept of growth as the very purpose of existence was seriously called into question. People demanded a "change of course." That same year, former salesman Erik Dammann of Norway published *The Future in Our Hands*. Two years later, he gathered three thousand people in a packed hall on the outskirts of Oslo to spread the word that it was time to abandon the ideology of growth. In 1972, Norway was one of the first countries in the world to appoint a minister of the environment, and ninety-three watercourses were assured permanent protection. Despite that, the growth arrows have continued to point ever upward over these fifty years, even in Norway, while trends related to nature have generally gone the opposite way. Global animal populations have more than halved on average over the same period, the time span for which data are available. Fifty years *before* 1972, which takes us back to 1922, our global footprint was already fairly visible, but the planet was still largely intact: there were still white spots on the map.

This period roughly covers my father's lifespan. He was born in 1924, into a society that had, in many ways, more in common with the Middle Ages than with the globalized, digitalized, materialistic, high-speed consumer society he left after a long life. People still used horses to plow fields and transport hay after cutting the grass with a scythe; most of their food came from roughly twelve acres of cultivated soil, rangelands, and fishing. Nothing was motorized, although electricity had arrived back then. My grandfather bought the island's first motorboat and, some years later, a splendid telephone apparatus to hang on the wall—whose number was 123. Roughly fifty years ago, these farms ceased operating, and only one stubborn holdout persisted with cattle farming and haymaking for a few more years. Efficiency took over, and there was no turning back. Those who grew up with toil were delighted by this development; although there may have been a certain melancholy in seeing the last animals sent off in the slaughter trucks, the world was moving on, to ever-greater heights and easier lives. My grandfather ate bread "by the sweat of his brow"—to quote the Bible he used to read—as farmers had done for ten thousand years before him, and his goal was for his children to get an education, join the modern world, and escape the drudgery he had experienced. Perhaps agriculture caught us humans like an eel trap: We renounced our freedom in exchange for safety and food—but also endless toil. Agriculture provided the foundations on which to build an ever-growing population, creating the need for ever-smarter farming methods, but we became like endlessly grazing ruminants. All our time was spent on food production, and we became trapped in a spiral of production and efficiency that only escalated with industrialization, the point of no return. From then on, progress in the sense of growth became an integral component—perhaps the most important component—of the human project.

I've always thought of development and growth as part of the human essence: the urge to advance, to see what lies around the next headland, or over the next blue ridge; to understand more, to solve ever more mysteries and problems. A kind of natural law of evolution for society, a development that wasn't necessarily for the best, but that led to innovation, new insights, and new limits to be overcome. I've thought of linear time and linear development as inevitable. After all, this is what drives me as a scientist, too. And growth has simply been an inescapable by-product. Yet the drive not just for growth but for ever-faster growth and constantly increasing efficiency is *not* a necessary part of existence. Humanity existed for thousands of years in which each day consisted of getting up in the morning and repeating exactly the same actions as the day before; and every generation did the same as the generation before them without having progress or efficiency gains as an inescapable motivation.

I'm not at all sure that I would find satisfaction or meaning in such a life, though, because I grew up in an age when development was an implicit part of existence. I'm no luddite; I find new technology impressive and enjoyable. I'm still fascinated by GPS, for example. That and other smart inventions are enough to make you proud to be human. Yet the problem with these things we now rely on—even though we had no idea we needed them until recently—is that they all make the carousel of consumption spin even faster. Another issue is that we are increasingly outsourcing thinking and judgment to mathematical optimization routines. *Algorithms* determine everything from the price of electricity to the top news stories, and the ads I'm exposed to. And they give us directions, distances, speed, and goals on our hikes—although some of the joy of achievement is lost along the way. I tend to take GPS with me on longish hikes in unknown terrain, but my standard equipment is still always map and compass.

I should mention that I want progress too, although in insight and reasoning rather than purchasing power. I have what I need, more than I need. A lot more, strictly speaking. The Norwegian philosopher Arne Næss, who founded "deep ecology," also coined the phrase "a rich life by simple means," which may have become something of a cliché but is a good motto all the same. It doesn't imply rejection of the future, but rather a different future; it's a question of replacing quantity with quality and slowing the speed of the hamster wheel a notch or two. In my daily life, I've gradually begun walking faster. I can't remember strolling, sauntering, or ambling for many years. I instinctively seek out the quickest route, then walk as speedily and efficiently as possible from A to B. Often to be on time for something, like a lecture or a meeting, although I generally don't need any reason at all, other than a desire to save or earn time that can then be spent on getting more done.

NOTICING THAT I'M walking at a heck of a lick even here in the mountains, I slow my pace. Just past the plane wreck, I find some reindeer tracks at last, but they're old. On the plus side, a whole herd has been here, although it's difficult to see how big it was. Other than on the highest ridges, where the reindeer lichen and star-tipped cup lichen have been kicked up, and where the wind has prevented the snow from concealing tracks and dung, most traces have been covered up. Reindeer often pass this way despite the sparse plant cover. It's not that reindeer love the nutrient-poor reindeer lichen or star-tipped cup lichen (which many people mistake for the former). No, what reindeer like best is lush grass, sedge grass in moist areas, herbs, and fungi, or heather, and willow or birch leaves, and they seek out protein-rich grazing in the form of fresh shoots. Lichen is the reindeer's equivalent of crofters' fare: the food that keeps it going through the winter when the mountains have little else to offer. As a lad, I'd heard that both types of lichen took seven years to regrow after you crushed them beneath your sole, so I used to feel a pang of guilt every time my hike led me over dry, lichen-covered ridges. Now I know that this is also the lichens' dispersal method: fragments can be blown to new places where they can establish themselves, and they're well able to withstand a spot of random trampling. Yet it's still striking how rapidly a path can be worn over the peaks.

The wind is picking up sharply and I consider turning back, but I want to reach my second goal first. It isn't far off. With the west wind at my back, I'm driven down the gentle slope that runs between Gråhøgda and Storkvien, the highest of the peaks in this area, before it ends up down in Imsdalen, the valley famous, among other things, for the wolf pair that ended their days here in 2001 after being *taken out* before they could establish themselves. I stop well before getting that far. Due south of Gråhøgda lies my destination: Borkebua. It is a cabin built of gray stone slabs and set in splendid isolation, with mountains and snowdrifts as far as the eye can see. Like Kluftbua, it is left open for anyone traveling in the mountains. Norway has a wonderful, trust-based tradition of leaving such cabins unlocked—spartan yet offering opportunities for shelter and a reasonably comfortable night. Stable-style doors are also a crucial detail when, as here, roughly two feet of densely packed snow blocks the entrance to the cabin. There's no need to clear a path to the door: all you need to do is open the upper half and crawl inside to take shelter from the wind, which has now become unpleasant even though the sun is shining.

It's high time for lunch, and I realize that I haven't been here for many, many years either. Back then, Dad and I sat in the doorway in late April beneath the baking sun and watched a sizable herd of reindeer grazing on the eastern flank of Storkvien. Dad was a fine fellow, no doubt about it. And whereas many people don't realize that about their own parents until it's too late, I already knew it in those days. He was, as I mentioned earlier, a typically frugal Western Norwegian with a strong sense of duty, but was generous all the same. He didn't offer praise lightly, but when he did give it, I knew I'd really earned it. We were on the same wavelength. He served as a practical and moral compass even in his absence: "What would Dad have done here?" He put his foot down when it came to unrealistic projects—like tracking a wolverine through deep snow and dense birch forest—but went along with my proposal to climb to the top of Storkvien even though it was late in the day and time to head home. So we went up to the top, approaching from the west to avoid scaring the reindeer. We looked down over Imsdalen toward the Rondane Mountains, which lay bathed in the low sun. The day was windless, perfectly still. Neither of us said a word. There was no need.

Today, by contrast, it's far from still and on my way back, the wind picks up in earnest—thirty-five, perhaps even forty-five miles per hour—but I'm warmly clad and it feels bracing to test myself against the wind. Countless ice crystals are burnished to roundness as they restlessly wander with the sun and wind at their backs, heading for lower-lying terrain where they can find repose. The sun glows palely through the driving flakes and the snow forms a shining circle around it. It's like wading through a shallow, silver-shimmering river. Several times, I feel like I'm skiing on the spot as I ascend the gentle slope, but when a rock appears to my right or left, I realize that I'm advancing steadily nonetheless. Then I become aware of a dark shape a few hundred yards away, up there to my left. It has a proper muzzle, doesn't it? The tail is harder to see, but the creature is undoubtedly moving steadily, parallel to me. And that can *only* be a wolverine. But as I reach for my binoculars, I realize that the "wolverine" is actually a rock after all, an optical illusion conjured up by the glittering river of snow flowing in the opposite direction.

MY THIRD GOAL here in the mountains is a rough talus slope on the southern side of a rocky outcrop. Here, roughly fifteen years ago, I followed a wolverine track that ran alongside other older prints, all of which vanished in among the rocks. It was the same time of year as now—the wolverine breeding season. Could it be a den? The wind is blowing harder and the day is drawing in, so I ought to turn back, but I carry on. I'm pushing it a bit here, but not irresponsibly so. I do turn back in the end, though: the visibility is too poor to search for the talus slope now—and besides, I only have the vaguest idea of where it was. Instead, I follow the lowest point in the terrain in a northwesterly direction, knowing that it will take me down toward the Breia and the river valley; this will offer me a safe route home if the wind ends up getting *really* strong. I've sought shelter here before during bad weather. And I *have* experienced proper gales elsewhere in these mountains. That was the first time I genuinely experienced the profoundly unpleasant sensation of a situation being out of control; not just that things *could* go badly wrong but that I *would* probably end my days up there in the mountains.

On that January day a storm with hurricane-force winds had descended on us unannounced, appearing out of the blue like an evil spirit. It rapidly became impossible to continue; the wind snatched away our map and even our compass, and the situation became dangerous. Luckily, my girlfriend—later my life partner—and I found a snowdrift behind a steep slope where we were able to dig a makeshift snow cave. The next day, after a cold, wet night in there, we tried to reach the cabin we'd been heading for, but there was zero visibility, and we eventually realized that this had been a mistake. Late in the afternoon of the following day, with the storm still raging, all hope seemed lost. This was before the days of GPS and cell phones. Our clothes were coated in a carapace of ice, we had no food left, everything froze, and everything was a white inferno. We couldn't make our way down to the forest because that would have meant walking directly into the wind, and our only hope was to find shelter or a miracle deeper in the mountains. Toward the end of the day, I pictured my children: it was early summer and they were walking beneath the cherry blossom down to the sea that glittered in the sun. I didn't feel any real anxiety at that point, just a peculiar resigned peace at the realization that life was over. Just when all hope seemed gone, a glimpse of a cabin revealed itself through the blizzard—or was it just another mirage? There were some large slabs of rock in the area that could easily be mistaken for a cabin, so our hope swiftly dimmed. But it was in fact a cabin. One of the windows was missing a shutter, so we were able to break in and reach shelter. We would live after all. Once inside the cabin, we managed to heat up one of the rooms, found some dry clothes in a closet, and happily lived off a can of fish balls for the next two days. After that, the storm died down at last and rescuers arrived on snowmobiles.

My girlfriend had proper mittens, so she was fine, whereas I had gloves—and that taught me a lesson. The most extraordinary blisters quickly formed on my frozen hands, and by the time we arrived at the hospital in a helicopter, my fingers were starting to turn black and lose all sensation. After a few days, the nails fell off and all feeling vanished; the doctors were uncertain about the fate of my dying digits but prepared me for the amputation of eight fingers all told. At that point, I recalled that

I had a colleague in Bergen whose area of research was leeches: Could they be my salvation? Before they start to suck blood, leeches inject their victims with an anticoagulant called hirudin, which can help stimulate the circulation. But before we had a chance to attempt this interesting experiment, my body fixed itself. Almost miraculously, life returned to the near-lifeless fingers, first in the form of welcome pain, then, gradually, a return of both movement and fingernails. A month later, I took my first skiing trip after the experience, fingers still stiff and bandaged inside warm mittens. It was late February, the sun had started to spread its heat; the trees dripped gently, the great tit's optimistic springtime song was audible for the first time, and I was intensely aware of how good it was to be alive.

So, yes, I have respect for the mountains; yet I have first and foremost felt safe out in nature—which is, of course, utterly indifferent to my wishes and feelings. It wishes me neither good nor ill. It isn't only a matter of what nature is, but just as much of what it is *not*. Nature makes no demands, has no expectations, and has become the only arena in which I am not driven by the clock or the need to carry out duties. It also gives me an opportunity to continue experiencing a glimmer of physical risk in an otherwise cushioned and overly safe existence in which all toil and peril have been eliminated. Society's vision of a risk-free life also implies a kind of collective lobotomization: domestic animals have smaller brains than their wild counterparts, so perhaps our cognitive capacity is also reduced by a lack of challenges. Nature can be dangerous, and pressing forward against the wind makes me feel alive—it's a bit unpleasant, a bit marvelous, and, potentially, a bit dangerous, but still well under control. I've had my share of winter experiences, and I always carry a bivouac bag with me on slightly longer trips off the beaten track, along with an extra set of woolen underclothes, extra woolen socks and mittens, and food and hot drinks. That's normally all you need to see you through a winter night. Maybe it won't give you a good night, but it's enough to ensure survival.

BACK AT THE CABIN, which has lost most of its hard-won heat over the course of the day, I'm physically exhausted, but in a good way. I light the stove, make a simple supper of fried reindeer shavings with bread on the side, and finish reading Fønhus by the stove. It ends badly for both Heine and Threefeet. The hunter follows the wolverine out onto a frozen lake in a strong gale, but while the animal can crouch down and secure its footing with its claws, Heine is seized by the wind, and neither skis nor poles can slow him down; a headlong hurtle ends in a talus, where his life ends too. Threefeet, meanwhile, continues to hunt reindeer for a few more years, until he is once more pursued by hunters who trap him in a talus where he seeks shelter, blocking the exits with rocks. For three weeks, an increasingly faint scratching is heard, and after that, Threefeet's life is over as well. It's an ending worthy of Fønhus, reflecting a kind of equality between human and animal. Both end their lives in the mountains, although Threefeet's demise is more difficult to shrug off, in a way; that slow death, imprisoned in the talus by people impervious to the idea that animals can also suffer. What's more, the wolverine was not merely an animal to them but a *monster.*

After finishing Fønhus, I go over to the outhouse to fetch more wood. I sit there quietly for a long time, listening out for mice. But the snow weasel must have scared them off: There's not even a hint of rustling in the woodpile this evening. The wind speed has slowed. Through the open door of the outhouse, I gaze once again at the overwhelming starry sky. Our own galaxy, the Milky Way, consists of several hundred billion stars, and the Milky Way is just one of maybe two hundred billion galaxies. Yet in the whole of the endless, cold, dark cosmos our planet may be the only one where there is life. One thing's for sure: neither people nor wolverines exist anywhere else in the universe.

Back by the stove again, I take out Henry David Thoreau's *Walden; or, Life in the Woods.* Thoreau was a nature lover, poet, and philosopher who didn't just rhapsodize romantically about nature from the comfort of his sofa but yearned to become part of it. "I went to the woods because I wished to live deliberately," he writes, "to front only the essential facts of life, and see if I could not learn what it had to teach, and not, when I came to die, discover that I had not lived. I did not wish to live what was not life, living is so dear."[7] Thoreau pursues his project by Walden Pond: "Near the end of March, 1845, I borrowed an axe and went down to the woods by Walden Pond, nearest to where I intended to build my house, and began to cut down some tall, arrowy white pines, still in their youth, for timber."[8]

Is it true that life is better out there? That life outdoors is more natural and therefore also *more correct*? No, Thoreau is definitely not that naive; what he is after is simply what the philosopher Arne Næss described as "a rich life by simple means." He too prizes solitude, but he is not a misanthrope. His main point is that life becomes richer out in nature, not just because of what nature is, but also because of what it is *not*. He thrives on solitude but has no objection to visitors, and he himself visits the village that isn't so far away from his self-built cabin in the woods on the shores of Walden Pond. "I have never felt lonesome, or in the least oppressed by a sense of solitude," Thoreau writes,

> but once, and that was a few weeks after I came to the woods, when, for an hour, I doubted if the near neighborhood of man was not essential to a serene and healthy life... In the midst of a gentle rain while these thoughts prevailed, I was suddenly sensible of such sweet and beneficent society in Nature, in the very pattering of the drops, and in every sight and sound around my house, an infinite and unaccountable friendliness all at once like an atmosphere sustaining me, as made the fancied advantages of human neighborhood insignificant, and I have never thought of them since.[9]

Some people, many I think, would find the idea of spending days or even hours in their own company totally unbearable, especially if they were cut off from their online social network. A cell phone detox is a genuine withdrawal, liable to cause as much anxiety and depression as any other form of cold turkey. Being alone in a cabin like this can seem twice as scary when you don't have cell phone contact either, in part because it reawakens our ancient fear of the dark. If we don't have a natural relationship to nature, the primeval fear that *something out there* is just waiting to get us resurfaces. No rational assurances can counter that, not even the knowledge that Norwegian nature is among the safest places anyone could spend time, even at night. And then comes the more existential angst—the fear of our own thoughts, the fear of fear, exacerbated, of course, by the absence of social contact. It's easy to take an ironic view of this, but I'm not inclined to be judgmental about the phenomenon of "cabin fright" just because I myself experience solitude, quiet, and darkness as islands in a sea of busyness and people. It's lovely to go for a few days without hearing anyone's voice, not even my own, but I wouldn't necessarily feel the same after a month. We humans are above all social creatures, and we have exacerbated this with a digital presence that makes our entire network continually accessible.

Cell phones have become both a physical and mental extension of our selves—to the extent that we risk our lives by texting as we walk across busy streets, can't resist checking that message while we're behind the wheel, and just have to answer the phone even when we're cycling down a steep hill with the kids on the back of our bike. For many people, an hour without this access feels like a black hole, and there appears to be no saturation point—other than the fact that there are only twenty-four hours in a day. One hundred and fifty times a day: according to Professor

Tor Wallin Andreassen of the Norwegian School of Economics, that's how often, on average, Norwegians check their mobile devices for notifications, even if they don't ping first. Our days are steeped in restlessness. I, too, have developed an addiction to my Mac, not just as a gateway to information but also as a doorway through which the thoughts trapped in my own head can pass, out into the entire world in principle. I still believe I could hold out for a good while as long as I had access to books. Although the problem with books is, of course, that they only enable the flow of information into our heads; they don't satisfy our growing need to convey knowledge. Or maybe not so much knowledge as opinions; it's hardly a stretch to claim that an imbalance has developed between knowledge in and opinions out. An experience may feel pointless if it can't be shared but remains trapped inside. The view from a peak has no value to a blind person unless someone else can communicate it verbally. But while that may offer a rudimentary experience, there is otherwise no view without an observer. Views, grandeur, and beauty are not inherent traits of a mountaintop; they require a sensory apparatus and a subjective observer. The view serves to bring joy to the person who feels its grandeur, but their joy at the experience remains *trapped* if it cannot be shared—or boasted about. What is the view worth without a selfie? It's a sensation familiar to every photographer: how the joy of a marvelous experience gives way to frustration if it cannot be immortalized and shared.

Fear of loneliness sits deep in us humans; there is no punishment worse than ostracism and isolation. How many couples stick together solely because the only thing worse than putting up with coupledom at the restaurant table is the idea of sitting there alone? No one wants to put their loneliness on display, especially because there is a social stigma attached to it. If we are going to turn to the natural as a guideline for living, it is clear that belonging—to the family, the flock, the clan, the village, or the society—has been a defining factor for both the self and the human experience. Yet I think I'd be capable of not just getting by but even thriving alone in the mountains for a year, perhaps after a preliminary social withdrawal. Beyond that, the hermit lifestyle is probably overrated, and even Thoreau's exile in the woods didn't last for his entire life. In fact, it was limited to just two years, two months, and two days, and involved intermittent human contact too. Some think that meant he was "cheating," but Thoreau wasn't trying to win some solitude contest. He was just pointing out how enriching it can be to go *into* nature, not just go *out* in it, and to be there for enough time to achieve a sense of belonging. We humans are social creatures who have evolved to be together, which is why the worst punishment is to be cut off from any participation in a community. A solitary life in the forest is therefore neither natural nor any more correct than a sociable life. But precisely because the social can be so *very* social, solitude is sometimes good as well. For Thoreau, the whole point of the exercise was to escape the gossip, din, and distractions of society, a need that is familiar to us all. I am all alone for just this week; I won't say a word, I won't meet anyone on my hikes, and the cabin stands in isolation, surrounded by the mountain forest and snow, in light or darkness, beneath sun or stars. It's delightful for a few days and, as I say, I think it would even be nice for a whole year, but I can't know that until I've tried.

Thoreau's yearning for nature and silence were not especially widespread in his own day, but *Walden* struck a chord with his readers, despite the almost antisocial message the author conveyed from his reclusive existence. The book's appeal lies in the fact that he was blessed with an exceptionally sensitive sensory apparatus, poetic talent, and a rare ability to communicate atmosphere with humor, which saved him from the pomposity that is all too common among nature poets. Thoreau's homage to nature, his defense of it, and his critique of the consumerist society of his age didn't just appeal in 1854 but has endured until the present day.

The original deep ecologists based their arguments less on a foundation of natural science than on an absorption in and feeling for nature. Yet their homage to nature was still primarily a response to urbanization and busyness, the anthill life, the trivialization of our existence, a life squandered on bread and circuses. And Thoreau was not the first.

The desire to devote oneself to nature rather than society was perhaps even more intensely expressed by lawyer Estwick Evans some thirty years before Thoreau's time in his *A Pedestrious Tour, of Four Thousand Miles, Through the Western States and Territories, During the Winter and Spring of 1818*. "I wished to acquire the simplicity, native feelings, and virtues of savage life; to divest myself of the factitious habits, prejudices and imperfections of civilization," Evans writes, "and to find, amidst the solitude and grandeur of the western wilds, more correct views of human nature and the true interests of man. The season of snow was preferred, that I might experience the pleasure of suffering and the novelty of danger."[10] In 1821, Evans visits a man of his own age, thirty-seven-year-old astronomer and geophysicist Christopher Hansteen, in Jotunheimen, Norway. Hansteen conveys the excellence of outdoor life with the same enthusiasm as Evans:

> The hypochondriac city-dweller, whose limbs' functions are half-arrested by his sedentary life, and whose spiritual existence is annihilated by the unsociability, egotism, and half culture of a half-grown town, should venture into the mountains once in a while. Just as the clean mountain air and the discomforts of the journey will stimulate the functions of his limbs, so will his mind be greatly cheered by the astonishing scenes of nature and the uncorrupted nature of the amiable mountain folk.[11]

This is, as the Norwegian nature writer Theodor Caspari drily notes a hundred years later, "an observation that, albeit expressed in the stiff language of the day, sums up the entirety of our modern approach to tourist life."[12] I leaf through a copy of *Nansen's Voice*, which Dad left here at the cabin. He was also an admirer of Fridtjof Nansen, though not unreservedly so. The title has a slightly bombastic, prophetic ring, but then again, Nansen didn't choose it himself. His elevation of outdoor living almost to a moral code has left a deep impression on Norway. Nansen's combination of the roles of scientist and explorer, humanist and existentialist, is beyond compare, as is his extraordinary career, which unfolded in parallel to his unswerving veneration for nature and his express desire for the simple and the natural. A rich life by simple means:

> Getting away from the crowds, away from the eternal tumult, the confusing din in which our life is all too frequently conducted—getting out into nature, out into the vast space. That, for me, is the greatest aspect of outdoors life. But we don't even achieve that if we set out in herds and walk the well-trodden paths, or cluster together in cabins, follow routes from one sanatorium to the next, or sail from one coastal resort to the next, and dance the evenings and nights away with lovely young ladies . . . The important thing, especially for us city folk, is precisely to get away from the familiar. This city life is antinatural, after all, and is certainly not what nature intended for us.[13]

Nansen is paying homage to the same freedom and simplicity extolled by Thoreau, Evans, Hansteen, and others, but what would his career have amounted to if he had devoted his *entire* existence to solitary wanderings in nature, if his thoughts and reflections had remained locked inside his skull? I think that would have been impossible for him. After all, Nansen most certainly did his fair share of dancing with lovely young ladies. His yearning for the wilderness, solitude, and simplicity was contingent on a hectic, multifaceted existence that sprang from an intense need to live life, even city life, and to create meaning in his life; and in every stage of his life, he felt compelled to communicate this. Nansen could not have lived a life like Thoreau's; not even Thoreau did that! Thoreau lived that life for a little over two years and probably would have found those two years considerably less meaningful if he hadn't also written about them—in detail.

Several times, in his yearning for the authentic and the simple, Nansen evokes Rousseau:

> Rousseau, you are needed now more than ever. In your day, it was mostly a small upper class that went astray; now the entire life of our society is in such a state that it can only go awry at railroad speed. A greater spirit must come that can change the train's course and lead us upward, to simplification—if not, humanity will go to the dogs.[14]

Exactly a hundred years after Hansteen made his observations, Nansen delivered a speech entitled "Friluftsliv": Outdoor life. "This city life is antinatural... Learn the intense joy of a simple life in nature, from which we stem after all, and not least, the joy of frugality."[15] In his journals, he constantly returns to the conflict he feels between duty and enjoyment, between the roles of scientist and citizen of the world, between choosing life in the wilderness or the salons. In the foreword to *The Sports Book* (1922) he writes:

> The development of culture has led human beings farther away from their natural life, has crammed them together in houses, offices, and factories; it has more or less made them into working, sedentary, writing, speaking, and sleeping machines. This "development"

> has crippled many a limb, has enthralled many a mind—far from the freedom of the forests and the wild plateaus.[16]

But this yearning for the simple life in the great outdoors has always been most intense among those living farthest away from that very nature, and who have had enough time and money to seek it out for purely recreational purposes.

Once, in our early youth—also nearly fifty years ago now—my childhood buddy Kjetil and I hiked more than fifty miles through the Norwegian mountains to visit his grandparents. Our real aim was of course to scale the mountains and peaks; the visit was just a pretext. We viewed our hike as a manly feat and expected a certain amount of recognition for our achievement. When we arrived, though, Kjetil's grandfather simply shook his head in puzzlement. He had spent a great deal of time hunting in the mountains—but walking over the mountains on a *hike*? What kind of an idea was that? Didn't our parents have enough money to buy us train and bus tickets? For him, nature was a place you went to harvest food. The mountains were splendid in their way, but most importantly, they were dangerous. There was a reason why one of the most beautiful peaks was called Styggehø—"Nasty Mountain."

Nature, especially in mountainous and open landscapes, has probably always evoked a certain sense of freedom. The hunting trip was both a source of excitement and an escape from the daily toil in the valleys. On top of that it provided food. My maternal grandfather, who belonged to the same generation, once took me to see the capercaillie courtship display. This was the one and only time of the year he went out in nature to do anything other than find food. Now and then, he might head into the deep forest right behind his house, but he would always take his shotgun so that he could supplement the family's diet. He was such a keen hunter that Mum would sometimes get sick of all the game suppers—hare and black grouse and wood grouse. Of course, this doesn't mean he didn't like being out there, that he didn't enjoy the freedom, the joy of getting away from it all. Yet the most *intense* catalyst for the love of nature is probably the absence of nature, the resultant yearning for nature, and it is therefore culturally conditioned.

Before 1820, barely anyone set foot in the mountains other than the odd reindeer hunter. When Jotunheimen was still terra incognita, two students in their early twenties, Baltazar Mathias Keilhau and Christian Peder Bianco Boeck, took a hike that makes my ramble with Kjetil 150 years later look like a walk in the park. Their aim was scientific: they were helping to map Norway. Back then, this region was a white spot on the map in all respects: the vast expanses of snow and glaciers they saw looking west from Kalvåhøgda mountain in mid-July 1820 were pretty different from the view I saw from the same spot in July 2020. The mountains were the same, of course, but the glaciers had shrunk considerably since their time. They were traveling without maps, likely with woefully inadequate equipment and food supplies, as well as few if any options for overnight accommodation. It was an enormously challenging journey westward in the wildest areas of the Jotunheimen Mountains, involving detours to numerous peaks; but it all worked out fine—the way it so often does. They probably experienced the same joy of discovery on their journey as Kjetil and I did on our hike. They must have been made of sterner stuff back then. And even though their activities had a scientific aim, and they, like Nansen, Amundsen, and Scott, were at pains to emphasize that this was not a mere adventure but a socially useful trek, they must surely have felt a thrill in their hearts when they reached the summit.

NATURE IS NOTORIOUSLY difficult to define, other than in opposition to all things human-made. Yet that is an artificial distinction. Everything in culture, even humanity itself, springs from nature, and much of what we most prize in cultivated landscapes—their openness, the variety of flowering plants, insects, and birds—is, well, human-made. Nature is more than untouched wilderness, which, incidentally, barely exists anywhere on the planet nowadays; but is a potted plant nature? The wolverine is nature, but is the wild reindeer nature and its domesticated counterpart not? Or are domesticated reindeer also nature, while sheep are not?

We humans have continuously engaged in a civilizing project aimed not just at conquering and subordinating nature but also at creating a *distance* from it, from the animal and the amoral. As we have come ever closer to achieving that aim, we have come to realize that a curse lies over it. We have cut the umbilical cord linking us to nature and been left with a profound sense of loss amid all the asphalt and concrete. But nature has enjoyed a renaissance, and the concept of the *natural* has now become a badge of honor, as the antithesis of the unnatural or the *artificial*. I'm talking here about a fundamental feeling that the former is good and the latter less so. If a person behaves naturally, there is by implication something authentic and honest about them, whereas an air of fakeness and mendacity clings to the artificial. In modern Western culture, "natural products" or "natural ingredients" are certain to sell better than those that are "artificial," based on the intuitive understanding that natural equals healthy and right, whereas artificial equals unhealthy or toxic. It is an interesting perception, especially considering that *nature itself* produces some of the most powerful toxins we know. Many plants and animals have an arsenal of potentially deadly substances they use for deterrence and self-defense. The belief that what is natural is also right strengthens as our distance from nature grows, and it is a cultural phenomenon. We need go back no further than the 1950s to find a time when the products of factories and laboratories were regarded as the very best you could put on or in you.

The concept of the natural (= nature) has the same appeal as the *authentic*. Authentic is good, inauthentic less so. Wood is authentic, plastic is inauthentic. Cross-country skiing in the forest is authentic, and for a long time it was important to use wooden skis: resistance to the switch from wooden to plastic skis was emotionally charged and heavy with symbolism. Wooden skis, which were associated with Nansen's treks across Greenland or to the North

Pole, Amundsen's "conquest" of the South Pole, and, later, the deep forest landscapes of long-distance cross-country races, were suddenly replaced with gaudy, "artificial" fiberglass skis, all too often foreign-made. Only wooden boats have a "soul," according to their owners. In the same way, wool in general and homespun in particular are viewed as especially authentic and good, whereas polyester and all kinds of petroleum-based products are inauthentic. Old log cabins are perceived as more genuine and definitely more beautiful than concrete buildings and gas stations, even though the loghouse was once new too, and all of these are as human-made as each other.

But how does this longing for—and marketing of—the original and the "authentic" fit in with a human project intent on marking its distance from nature? The answer is complicated but also reflects a change over time. While the desire to distance ourselves from nature stems from a period in which human beings felt small and vulnerable in the face of a vast, overwhelming, and dangerous nature, the yearning to return to nature is a more recent phenomenon triggered by our all-too-successful attempt to cut the umbilical cord connecting us to our origins. It may also stem from a yearning for rootedness in an ever-changing world. A hundred years ago, Indigenous peoples were perceived by white people as barbarians, whereas they are now held up as charismatic and "authentic," and many believe they possess profound insights lost to people living in postindustrial consumer economies.

If we like log cabins and flower meadows better than storage facilities and parking lots, it's because they give us a sense of harmony and beauty. If a day in the mountains brings us more happiness and peace of mind than a day at the mall, it's also because, as I previously mentioned, the experience of nature is not just about what nature is, but also what it is *not*. There is an element of nostalgia at play too. If we like old cultivated landscapes, this is partly for aesthetic reasons, and partly because they represent something enduring and constant. If we see grandeur in untouched nature, this feeling also stems precisely from our awareness of the untouched and the natural, without our being able to explain why the untouched, as such, has this appeal. A bit like E. O. Wilson, I can offer a rational explanation for my fascination with the wolverine, but I have no need to. It's enough that they exist: both the fascination and the wolverine.

Extolling *the natural* as *the right* is a debatable position: nature is definitely not a moral compass. Should natural preferences and reactions be prioritized precisely because they are natural? This is a fundamental question of moral philosophy. Unless we adopt the highly unscientific view that human nature is irrelevant (that we are in some sense "purely" cultural products—or have more in common with angels than animals), we can claim that the origins of many of our actions, pleasures, woes, and preferences lie, to a greater or lesser extent, in our own inner nature. However, nature is not moral or immoral but, strictly speaking, simply amoral. It only has the answers that are biologically right, and what is biologically right may well be morally wrong. If we consider ancient methods of punishment—blood vengeance and medieval barbarism—we can count ourselves lucky for the humanizing influence of norms and regulations. And, necessarily, answers that have been right from time immemorial can suddenly become wrong; strictly speaking, evolution only has yesterday's answers. Giving in to the urge to eat fat, salt, and sugar, for example, is inadvisable in an everyday existence that constantly thrusts an excess of all these things upon us.

We cannot derive an ethical "ought" from a biological "is," warned the analytical philosopher G. E. Moore, who called this "the naturalistic fallacy." What is natural is therefore not right on ethical or moral grounds. Is a day in the mountains "righter" than a day spent sitting in a café? Well... It's probably righter from a strictly physical point of view, and, for many of us, from a mental perspective too. *Morally*, however, we cannot claim that the mountain hike is necessarily righter. Our hike may have been an equipment-heavy ego trip during which we boosted global CO_2 emissions on our way to the mountains (as is increasingly the case with mountain hikes), whereas we may have cycled to the café to discuss the big issues and the planet's salvation. However, it is surely fair to claim that a day in the mountains or forest is *generally* righter than a day at the mall. Not because either of the activities is intrinsically nobler than the other, but because the mall is the very high temple of consumerism, whereas the frugal brand of outdoor life that prevailed until the 1980s falls within the bounds of a sustainable lifestyle. Indeed, it was the very essence of it, as advocated by Thoreau, Nansen, and Næss. And that is still the point of outdoor life for people who seek out nature itself. However, outdoor life has become the foe of nature in some respects, since so many of those who seek escape from the tumult of the big city on the weekend achieve their dream of nearness to nature via panoramic views of the mountains from an outsized holiday cabin accessible by all-season highways and other comforts that take a toll on land and resources. And the endless stream of ads for every conceivable kind of outdoor product shows how tight a hold the tentacles of the market have on a space that should be free from the iron grip of economics.

ONLY GLOWING EMBERS remain in the stove when, legs somewhat stiff, I eat a slice of brown cheese, brush my teeth beneath the stars, and call it a night at last. I don't remember falling asleep and once again I enjoy nine hours of deep sleep—which I never normally do. The absence of light, the absence of noise, the absence of time. During the last hour, I dream the way I often do in the morning: peculiar short stories that are barely coherent, their plots drawn from thin air, involving places and people I've never seen before. The sleeping brain churns out stories that are seemingly improvised, yet still manages to give the dream some kind of meaningful cohesion.

Dreams are a mystery on a par with consciousness, and the two are interlinked. Where does the brain source the raw materials for these short stories—sometimes entire novels—with their rich casts of characters, their logic, their colors? *Why* do we make up dramas in our sleep? Need there be a rational, Freudian explanation, or could it just be our brain at play now that it's been let off the leash? A playful level of consciousness that escapes the auditing eye of the rational mind, the superego, during sleep?

Dreams always explode the framework of a regular day, offering more color, unknown people, exotic experiences. On this particular night, I find myself in many unfamiliar places but ultimately arrive via some incomprehensible route at a train station. There are masses of people here. It's winter, but suddenly switches to summer. A red-clad woman appears, her hair wet from a boat trip. She smiles. In some peculiar fashion, the dream writes Dad into the story at the end. I'm on the edge of consciousness when my dreams invent a new story. Not an exotic and logically incomprehensible short story this time, but one set on Dad's childhood farm on Hessa, the island on the west coast of Norway that gave us our surname and which was also my childhood paradise. There's always a certain melancholy to these dreams that turn up now and then, albeit in different guises. The landscape with barn, boathouse, and open fields down to the fjord has now vanished beneath houses and highways, and I know this in my dream, in a way that refashions the farm and landscape into something different yet still recognizable. We are all younger in these dreams; my own children are small, but I know in the dream that Dad doesn't really belong here, that he too is gone. He always has slightly hazy contours. I used to have dreams like this about my sister Marit for many years after her death, but now she has also vanished from my dreams. Unfortunately, reality has imposed sanctions on the night's fantasies and tales. Although the dreams roused a certain melancholy, they still kept Marit alive in my memory.

I really ought to have dreamed I met the wolverine out there in the mountains this time, but there's nothing I can interpret as a wolverine in the dream; and in any case by the time I drink my morning coffee, it has dissipated into a rudimentary black-and-white vestige of the colorful tale that existed just minutes earlier.

ON THIS MORNING, I ski due south along a stretch of bog and past a steep rock face that ends in a frozen lake. Up there on the cliff is a big nest made of twigs and, as a boy, I climbed up this rock face, all the way to the nest, while a pair of rough-legged buzzards screeched above me. Two fluffy chicks lay in the nest. It was a stupid thing to do in every possible way, and I later became seized with anxiety at the thought that I might have scared off the adults. I had no peace of mind until I checked from a safe distance later in the spring and spied the two chicks through my binoculars, almost airworthy on the edge of the nest. Perhaps some new rough-legged buzzards will nest here sometime soon, the tenth-generation descendants of the ones that nested here back then. It's still a bit early in the year, so I'll have to check again in spring.

I wade down a steep hillside to a long, narrow tarn, where a pair of ptarmigans suddenly fly up—followed by another two. White with black wing feathers. These are the first ptarmigans I've spotted during the days I've been here, and they have left their crisscrossing tracks around willows and dwarf birches beside the frozen lake. It's unusual to see ptarmigans down here in the forest, but maybe the wind has also forced them to seek shelter. I continue into the mountains but remain in the forest of downy birch. Has the wolverine also made its way down from the bare mountain, or is it lying buried in a snowdrift, or in a talus, waiting for milder weather and better hunting conditions? It's hard going, wading through the forest; only on the larger bogs is the snow packed hard enough for me to more or less glide on its surface. So I head down toward the great expanses of bogland that extend into the bare mountain. In late spring, there are cranes here, always in pairs. You can hear their trumpet blasts a long way off and they nest by a small pond out in the middle of the bog. But they are shy birds, so I have always resisted the temptation to visit the nest. Even as a boy, when I was obsessed with spotting as many types of bird eggs as I could in the course of the season, I observed the cranes from a respectful distance. It had been impressed on me that they were shy and rare, and besides they looked like the aristocrats of the bird world, dressed in gray coats and striding over the bogland on lanky legs. They had a lofty air, these birds, and seemed elevated above the rest of the nature around them—an impression somehow enhanced by the fact that cranes are monogamous. Crane couples stay together for life.

Swans are somewhat similar: they too have that strange blend of the graceful, the commanding, and the pure—and also remain faithful until death do them part. One of the most striking sights I have ever seen here in the mountains was a pair of swans frozen into the early fall ice of the remote Breitjønn tarns, surrounded by barren land and peaks. Both were dead, their necks and heads beneath the ice. Had one of them frozen stuck first—perhaps it grew weak and had to stop off here during migration and was unable to go any farther? Did its loyal mate then choose to remain by its side, so they could await death together? It was disquieting to see these two great white birds, frozen solid into the new, mirrorlike ice here in the mountains; and this swan lake tragedy in the frosty, magnificent setting made a peculiarly powerful impression on me. Soon the raven, the fox—and, yes, maybe even the wolverine—would return the swans to the cycle of nature.

Today, too, I see little more life than those four ptarmigans. But the sun shines on the snow all the way, and I think of the unique happiness that this gives me, and of what Thoreau wrote about it in his day.

> The sun at length rises through the distant woods... melting the air with his beams... We step hastily along through the powdery snow, warmed by an inward heat... What fire could ever equal the sunshine of a winter's day...?... Standing quite alone, far in the forest, while the wind is shaking down snow from the trees, and leaving the only human tracks behind us.[17]

Back at the cabin, I am in a state of happy exhaustion, but I pack my bag in sorrow. I so wish I could spend the rest of the winter here and experience the transition from late winter to early spring, almost imperceptible until, one mild morning, the new season suddenly explodes into song with the arrival of bullfinch and redwing, the bare patches spread, and the wet snow heaves a deep sigh, realizing the battle is lost for now. But I am not Thoreau: I am a prisoner of our hectic modern life. I am caught up in duties, and my stolen days here in the mountain are over for now. Before I lace up my bag and shut the door behind me, I put my watch back on and switch off airplane mode on my cell phone.

SOME DAYS LATER, I'm sitting in my office peering out of the window when a message drops into my inbox from a friend with a cabin slightly northeast of my own. He's gotten wind of my quest to track down a wolverine and sends me a few envy-inducing photographs of wolverine tracks from a cross-country skiing trip in mid-March. Walking on a hard crust thinly coated in fresh snow, the animal has crossed an open area on its way toward a stand of downy birch trees. In the background, the birch forest climbs some way up toward a mountain before abandoning its ascent. After that, the mountain takes over, white and bathed in sun. The tracks look a bit like bear prints. A distinct heel imprint, the pad in front of that, then five toe pads and the toes, with their distinct claw marks. The tracks in the picture lead toward the open forest of downy birch.

There's an unmistakable shimmer of spring on the bare trees outside the window of the room where I'm sitting, and this photo of the wolverine tracks on the snow rouses an intense yearning in me to be there, to follow those tracks into the sun on silky smooth snow, never stopping until I see the wolverine, a dark manifestation of a wild animal in all that whiteness. It's no mean effort to track a wolverine, which is like a machine seemingly capable of walking forever. An acquaintance tracked a male wolverine for five days and nights as it headed for the sea, well outside its own habitat. It roamed from the Hardanger

Plateau almost all the way to Kristiansand on the southern coast, a distance of close to 150 miles; there, it stood on a hill and gazed out over the ocean, perhaps the first of its kind ever to do so, probably wondering what this flat, twinkling eternity could be. Not unlike the snowy plains on a sunny day on the plateau. Then it turned. It was one of two wolverines who took it in turns to patrol the Hardanger Plateau and the enormous stretch to the mountain areas farther south over a period of ten years, vainly searching for a female wolverine. Both were "taken out" in the end.

The wolverine's reputation as a wanderer and a perpetual motion machine has frequently been confirmed. One young wolverine, identified via fecal DNA analysis, started its voyage in Älvdalen, Sweden, not far from the eastern Norwegian municipality of Engerdal. The following winter, it was found to have made its way to the southwestern Norwegian mountains before going back east the way it came and being registered near the Swedish border a month later. A free spirit, perhaps, but also constantly on the move, simply for survival's sake. Possibly the most impressive trek recorded involved a wolverine that was registered in the very northernmost part of Norway in 2013 before going all the way to the western coast nearly 1,250 miles away, where it was shot dead two years later.

DESPITE MY DESPERATE longing to return to the mountains, I don't manage to get away until a month and a half later, in mid-April. There isn't a breath of wind, and the days are starting to get properly warm, although the nights are still frosty so there's a rock-hard crust on the snow in the mornings. As usual, I arrive late in the evening, but the dense darkness of winter has now given way to a deep blue sky with an optimistic pale blue horizon to the west. I wake at the crack of dawn the next morning and prepare my packed lunch with feverish zeal before gobbling three slices of bread washed down with a few cups of black coffee. I normally set store by the slowness of life in the mountains, but when the spring sunshine is baking the ground outside, it's crucial to make the most of the morning hours. I catch myself thinking how similar the love of nature feels to other forms of love after a long period of separation and yearning—although, of course, I realize that my yearning for nature is unrequited.

It is already warm in the sunshine when I brush my teeth on the doorstep of the cabin. The redwing must have arrived the day before, and I can also hear the fieldfare. Here's a strange thing: two of the most common thrushes, the song thrush and the blackbird, are equipped with a wonderful, almost melancholically beautiful song, and the redwing isn't far behind. Few things give me such a powerful sense of spring as the morning song of the redwing. Yet the fieldfare hasn't the slightest singing talent, and the sound it makes when it flies off is more like a cacophony of rusting hinges. Even so, this sound makes me happy too, because of its associations with spring, and with the great passion of my childhood and youth. We humans are collectors, and what I collected was birds' eggs. Not the physical eggs—just sightings of them. After a while, I began to write down all my observations, along with detailed notes about dates, eggs, and the chicks I found in an ever-increasing number of bird boxes. My record was somewhere around forty different birds' eggs in a single season, from the boreal owl in April via all kinds of different tits that nested in the bird boxes to the rock ptarmigan in the Jotunheimen Mountains in midsummer. For a while I made a habit of climbing up to every single fieldfare nest I spied—even when dressed in my Sunday best for Norway's Constitution Day, and even though there is remarkably little difference between one fieldfare nest and another: they're always lined with straw, and always contain five or six greenish eggs with brown speckles. Incidentally, the song thrush doesn't just have the forest's sweetest song; it also has the forest's most beautiful eggs, laid in the forest's most elaborate nest. Blue eggs speckled with black in a nest whose bowl looks as if it was fashioned by a skilled wood turner: a perfect laminated wooden bowl. One such nest that I found after nesting season—probably abandoned, no eggs—is still at the cabin. I sawed off a little cleft branch that was a suitable size for the nest and glued the whole thing to a wooden pedestal, and there it still stands on a shelf above my bed, along with a bullfinch nest. It was the first thing I saw when I opened my eyes this morning. I took it down and ran my index finger along the base of the bowl, which is still as smooth as ever after all these years. A masterpiece.

The black grouse are making a commotion below the cabin when I set off. But the display itself is over, and this is just some half-hearted courtship going on in the top of a fir tree down by the bog; besides, it's best not to approach the bird on skis that are liable to skid on the hard snow. So I take it easy skiing down the hills from the hut, then pole across the bogland and skate through the sparse birch forest toward Breistølen again. Skate-skiing through the birch forest on the crusted springtime snow in the morning sun gives me an indescribable feeling of lightness. There's barely any friction and the speed is intoxicating as I skate, slaloming between the white tree trunks. By the time I've passed the summer farm and I'm heading up through the birch forest where I sank into the deep snow a month ago, I'm advancing effortlessly. Of course, these are terrible conditions for spotting tracks: even the cloven hooves of a moose barely leave a mark on the crust, and any tracks left after the snow softens up during the day rapidly become indistinct and impossible to identify. After a while, I cross some tracks that *might* have been a wolverine's but also—more probably—a fox's. The bare patches eat into the snow from day to day, and the southern slope of Øverlihøgda is mostly clear of snow now. It's still too early to eat my packed lunch, but this is a fine place to sit. I pick up a sweetish, fresh scent, one of the finest aromas I know: sun-warmed heather in springtime or in the wake of a light drizzle.

I lie down in the heather at the foot of a cliff and stay there a while watching two ravens playing high up in the sky. Shouldn't they already be nesting down in Breia gorge by now? That's where the river forms its first proper waterfall, which cascades into a black pool between the walls of the gorge. The next waterfall and pool are even wilder. On one side, a sheer rock face looms, and this is where the raven has its airy nest. Or one of them. Perhaps these are last year's chicks, now young adults, relishing the liberty of carefree flight before the serious business of adult life claims them next year. I hear the characteristic whirring of a male ptarmigan nearby. At this time of year, you can get pretty close to them, but I don't manage to spot this one. Even the sound of it makes me happy, though, and I picture it to myself, tripping through the heather, brown summer feathers replacing the white, a bright red comb above its eyes—high on spring, happy, and feeling that life is good.

As I press on, I find the snow is already beginning to give way where juniper bushes lie beneath. Days like these are treacherous for a cross-country skier. You're tempted far out onto the plateaus by the morning crust; at first the going may be a bit tough on the night-hardened snow, but then there's a perfect period when the topmost inch or so has been softened by the sun. A bit later in the day comes the transition period when the north-facing slopes can still save you, but after that the fun stops, and the heedlessness of the morning exacts a high price when your skis sink deep into the snow and every step is an ordeal. In other words, I don't have the whole day to play with and don't have time to search for tracks beneath every single cliff and talus—or an opening in the snow between the rocks like the one I found here once. I can't be all that far from the talus, but there's little snow and no tracks, and I'm already starting to break through the crust. I follow shady, north-facing leeward slopes, seek out couloirs between bare patches, and descend into the river valley. Here, the snow has formed drifts after a long winter of northerly winds, and this offers a safe route back down beside a river that is now shrugging off its winter guise. The Breia has rid itself of most of the snow and ice cover and is thundering ever more confidently down toward Gudbrandsdalen and on to the large lake, Mjøsa. There's a very particular sense of achievement to be had from springtime skiing, with its constant search for routes and couloirs. But there's no mercy on the leg from the last bog, up the hills to the cabin. The snow is rotten, and the crust is treacherous. Only short stretches offer snow capable of carrying my weight. When at last I arrive at the cabin after stomping the last mile uphill, skis plunging through the rotten wet snow into the juniper undergrowth below, I am *utterly exhausted*. Safely ensconced in the cabin, I collapse on a chair and sit there for a long while before getting started on supper. This low-lying mountain area is no place to hang around. I need to go higher into the mountains—and I have both a plan and an appointment.

EARLY THE NEXT MORNING, I pack and head on toward the peaks I see looking northward from the cabin window, the Rondane Mountains. North of these peaks is where I'm going. There are some cranes on the fields farther up in Gudbrandsdalen; these graceful birds know that the bogs in the mountains will soon be open and ready for a new season. In the far north of Gudbrandsdalen, I veer off, starting up the sides of the valley, past log cabins and storehouses, past a few places where the sheep have already been let out into the spring pastures, and continue into the mountains. On the outer edges of the Rondane Mountains, just where the last crooked downy birches give way to the bare mountain, I meet two people who really *know* about wolverines, Eivind and Espen of the Norwegian Nature Inspectorate. I contacted Eivind a few weeks back and we picked out some dates when they would be going into the mountains and I could tag along. The temperature dipped slightly below freezing last night, but warmer weather is on its way, much warmer weather today. We have only a small window of opportunity, even at this high altitude. Our destination today is a possible breeding area. Wolverine populations are controlled in Norway, so it's important for the inspectorate to have a good overview of both animal and den numbers. Even snowmobiles have difficulty puzzling out a route between the bare patches; I'm hitching on the back of Eivind's snowmobile, trying to read the terrain so that I'll know when to lean right or left, depending on the angle of the slope or whether he has to turn.

On our way to the wolverine den, we pass an Arctic fox's den that has been abandoned for several decades, although the den complex is still clearly visible after many years of use and soil fertilization. The Arctic fox is one of the animals that benefits from the wolverine's presence: there are always some leftovers from a wolverine's meal—for the same reason, this fox also follows polar bears in the north. I don't know whether a decline in wolverines pushes down the Arctic fox population, but it is a fact that the latter species has been absent from this mountain region for many years, even though it is protected. The most important reason is probably that life is tough for the Arctic fox's main prey, small rodents, so there are long gaps between population peaks. The climate is the culprit in this case, but as long as there are reindeer here, the wolverine will remain, to the extent that we let it. We "take out" so many that the population remains barely above the level assumed to be the viable minimum.

On this crust, we're soon a dozen miles into the valley, let's call it Wolverine Valley, where we hope that breeding is underway. Here, too, the north wind has deposited snowdrifts on the descent into a valley not unlike the one the Breia River runs through, if somewhat larger. We park the snowmobiles some way off and cover the last stretch toward the edge on foot. In the snowdrift beneath a stand of birches, there's a hole in the snow. Large enough for a wolverine and dug by one. A wildlife camera is set up here and we excitedly look through the images, which reveal that both male and female wolverines have visited regularly throughout the late winter. Two days ago, a male wolverine stood by the entrance and rubbed up against the birch twigs and the den entrance. There's a paw print here, not quite fresh, but the scent of wolverine emanates from the opening. All the earlier signs indicate breeding, but no one can say for sure if there are any wolverine cubs in a hollow beneath the snow someplace on this slope. The mere possibility, even probability, of it is exciting, though. Wolverine tracks crisscross the valley below, but the arrival of the sun and warmth yesterday has played havoc with them, perhaps as recently as today. From the valley floor, we can see a fresh track running down to the right-hand side of the opening. It continues straight down across the snowdrift, turns left, and vanishes at the point where the crust is still hard as glass.

Perhaps it's this same trail we pick up again on the other side of the valley—this time a truly fresh track. Despite its broad paws, the wolverine has broken through the crust, which is now starting to thin; only in one spot is there a sharply defined imprint of the wolverine paw on the surface. It is five inches or so from the front toe pad to the carpal pad on the heel of the forepaw. Perhaps it's a male, but if so, it isn't an especially large one, according to Eivind, who reckons that the conclusive dividing line between the sexes is somewhere around 4.5 inches; that said, the behavior displayed by the tracks as well as breadth and gait also hint at whether a male or female wolverine has passed this way. Eivind, who is local and has tracked countless wolverines over the years, can spot this kind of thing, but I most definitely can't. The wolverine track I measured in 1972 was 6.5–7 inches, so—with the proviso that my measurements may have been imprecise—it must have been a sizable male. I follow the tracks up the side of the valley on foot: they vanish where the snow crust lies in the shade but reappear somewhat higher up, where they turn right beneath a crag. The wolverine has walked effortlessly here in this steep terrain, barely leaving claw marks on the hard crust, whereas I, without crampons or an ice axe, reach a point up on the side of the valley where I can no longer gain purchase. I peer down at the rocks that lie below, where the glass-hard slope ends, remember how Heine Juvet's wolverine hunt ended, and beat a prudent retreat to the valley floor. Fifty years ago, loose snow—and Dad—forced me to abandon the wolverine's track; this time it's the snow crust. The wolverine would barely register those factors as a challenge; it's perfectly capable of climbing up and down sheer icy rocks and steep mountainsides. It is at home here.

When the sun is at its zenith, we find a sunny, south-facing ridge covered in heather that is already warm and dry. We boil some coffee over a campfire in a sooty kettle, eat some locally sourced cured moose heart, and all agree that life could be a great deal worse. And we talk about the wolverine. It is probably breeding somewhere around here, as the crisscrossing tracks indicate—but where? There are plenty of snowdrifts, talus slopes, and couloirs, and we have visited some of the ones that have previously served as breeding grounds, but with no success. There's food here too. From our vantage point, our binoculars allow us to pick out a herd of bucks on the plateaus, close to a hundred animals.

The wolverine hole is in a beautiful spot, at the top of the slope with a southern prospect—into the mountains to the west, where reindeer herds also roam; down to where the valley broadens to the east; the peaks of the mountains to the south. A kingdom. I constantly wonder what a wolverine thinks about this view. Perhaps it doesn't think so very much, but I believe that it *feels* this is a good place to be on a sunny April day. An animal as advanced as the wolverine has the same signal substances in its brain as we do, which means we also share some of the same fundamental emotions. Not that I think it reflects much about past and future, about the meaning of life and that kind of thing; but, like all mammals, the wolverine has an emotional register not entirely unlike our own. And in contrast to its image as a legendary killing machine, the wolverine is also playful. Play is surplus energy and joie de vivre. Down the steep snow slope not far away from the opening there are fresher tracks, and here the wolverine has slid down before setting off on foot again. There are more or less anecdotal reports of wolverines—especially the young—sliding down snowy hillsides in a way that is suspiciously reminiscent of play. In the great work about Norway's mammals that he nearly managed to complete before his death in 1912, zoologist Robert Collett writes:

> Just like otters and badgers, wolverines take pleasure in sliding down slopes on their backs or stomachs. Sometimes, you can even see them in the spring, sledding down glaciers for long stretches of time; they hurl themselves on their backs, slide down headfirst, then run back up again and can keep this up for hours on end. The cubs play like puppies.[18]

Otters and badgers are, incidentally, also mustelids, relatives of the wolverine. From a rational biologist's perspective, this sledding game may be no more than a cleaning exercise to get rid of parasites rather than play for play's sake. Yet it has been proven beyond any doubt that the wolverine's relative, the otter, plays for the pleasure of it, just like us. So why shouldn't the wolverine do the same, assuming that it's well fed and healthy, its young are safe in the den, the spring sunshine is warming the snowy slopes, and it feels good to be alive?

When I started out as a biology student, we had a stall in the basement of the biology building that contained an ever-changing menagerie of animals, the most fascinating of which were the lynxes. Before my time, it had also housed wolves and polar bears, for the purpose of various physiological studies, and, for a period, two wolverines. What they were doing there, I never found out. Morten, the man who always—that is, from 1970 to 2015—ran the stall and had a kind of legendary status among field biologists, had a real way with animals. He would walk calmly into the wolverines' enclosure and was eventually able to scratch them behind the ears. And wolverines brought up in captivity can often display the playfulness of dogs, if not their devotion. Yet they do not have the social instincts of the herd animal.

Zoologist Douglas H. Chadwick writes about this in *The Wolverine Way*, one of the most intense and erudite yet subtle books I have read about wolverines. It is a quite magical account of a multiyear research project in the craggy mountains of Glacier National Park, Montana, run by Chadwick and his colleagues. Now, while competition within wolverine-themed literature can hardly be said to be tough—it is a tiny niche, after all—Chadwick's book, with its subtle humor and understatement, also scores high in the genre of wilderness literature in general. He leaves the reader to deduce that pursuing the wolverine on foot up and down the steep hills and precipices in this terrain is an arduous task.

Chadwick cites a colleague who once observed a wolverine "dancing" to lure some caribou. The wolverine and the herd had been eyeing each other from what, for the caribou, was a safe distance. But then the wolverine started making some peculiar movements, before lying down on its back, waving its legs in the air, and rolling around. This eccentric behavior piqued the curiosity of the caribou—could they be witnessing their archenemy's death throes? They came closer and closer to watch the wolverine's capers, but as soon a calf got within close range, the wolverine made a lightning-fast leap in its direction—and missed. It then repeated its bizarre dance moves and maneuvers and, once more, the curious caribou drew closer; again, the wolverine pounced, but the caribou were too far off and escaped. Eventually, the wolverine realized the battle was lost, shrugged off its disappointment, and wandered away.

A short video clip I happened across shows a wolverine swimming across a lake at breakneck speed, trying to cut off a deer that is approaching from a different angle. Once it gets to the other side, the wolverine runs ashore, glances at the deer, which has not yet noticed it, and clearly lays a swift plan of action. It sneaks across a snowy slope and takes up a position behind some large rocks. Here it lies, pulse presumably racing, waiting for the deer to reach dry land and unwittingly approach it across the same slope. At the last minute, however, the deer senses danger and swims off once more.

In a brief digression, Chadwick talks about his visit to Dale Pedersen, a man who had—among many other animals—ten to twelve wolverines that he kept in an enclosure in a large natural area. Chadwick notes in astonishment how even he, a wolverine expert, found his perception of the wolverine as a grumpy, aggressive loner challenged when he saw the animals running around at play, climbing the trees like overgrown squirrels and tumbling around in groups. His surprise was hardly diminished when Pedersen invited him into the wolverine enclosure and the animals approached him like dogs, sniffing eagerly at the legs of his pants and allowing Pedersen to scratch them under the chin. All of them had been born there or arrived there when small and had become socialized. The story reminds me of Dmitri Belyaev's breeding project involving foxes—or rather, Arctic foxes, which are a species related to the red fox. Belyaev's aim was to work out how and how fast domestication could take place, using one hundred females and thirty males obtained from Russian fur farms. The animals he selected at the outset were the ones that seemed friendliest to humans. After pursuing a strict selection process, whereby the "tamest" and most playful foxes were systematically chosen to continue the line, Belyaev was amazed to discover that it took only a few generations for the foxes to become strikingly like dogs not only in temperament and devotion but also in appearance—with shorter snouts, floppy ears, broader heads, and curly tails. And we all know about the taming of the wolf, from the most hated and feared predator to 450 breeds of dogs in every conceivable shape and size.

Wolverines are also kept in zoos, where I've seen them myself. Behind a high mesh fence topped by electrified barbed wire. It wasn't the worst animal prison I've seen, but that's only because there are some really appalling ones. Tigers that, despite a few trees and the illusion of nature, are serving a life sentence without any opportunity to live out their natural life. Polar bears imprisoned behind concrete with a pool to cool down in. Chimpanzees with climbing frames but otherwise entirely surrounded by concrete and gawped at by pointing people who notice the similarities between themselves and the animals without seeing their own barbarity. Many of these animals roam restlessly or have given up and lie around listlessly waiting for feeding time. The ones who were born there won't have any memory of what has been stolen from them; they are unwitting victims of shifting baselines. This is the world as they know it. Just as people born in prison may be contented with the status quo if this is the only reality they know. Indeed, Thoreau would have claimed that, to some extent, many people are victims of a self-imposed imprisonment, through their failure to go out into nature and experience a free life beyond the city streets. And while it's true that modern zoos offer better living conditions, the premise remains the same. The animals are robbed of most opportunities to live their lives to the full; they are there on our terms, for our entertainment. We shake our heads over the olden days with their exhibitions of excessively hairy individuals and other specimens from the human cabinet of curiosities. I believe that a hundred years from now, we will be ashamed of our equivalent treatment of advanced mammals. In fairness, it must be said that modern zoos provide animals with totally different living conditions, and in some cases such institutions can be a species' last line of defense against extinction. Breeding in zoos with a view to reestablishing a species in nature or shoring up dwindling populations may justify the imprisonment, but we could also consider sparing the animals this humiliating life support system and representing them instead with a memorial plaque, a testament to human arrogance and stupidity.

I have generally felt an intense discomfort and sorrow after my few visits to zoos, and my encounter with the wolverines in the enclosure was no exception. It wasn't that I believed that the animals behind the fence were troubled by a sense of yearning and loss, since they had been born there and had no memories of lost liberty. They had a patch of nature to frolic in, with trees, soil to dig in, artificial dens, a few places where they could escape the human gaze. They were probably born in captivity or arrived here as cubs, and this was their world. One of them came over to the fence and observed me with crushing indifference; I might as well have been a tree stump. I tried to make eye contact and read something into its gaze, but it was impossible. Yet it didn't seem resigned in the way the tiger or polar bear had been. Another wolverine had settled with its back against a fallen tree trunk, forepaws out to the side and hind legs splayed. Like a tourist on a sunbed. It was simply impossible to guess what was going through its head—if anything at all. It clearly wasn't suffering, but neither was it living life on the terms natural to a wolverine. It was tamed and transformed into something else. No opportunity to roam across the plateaus from horizon to horizon; no opportunity to hunt reindeer in the dawning light of a January day in the mountains; no opportunity to mate and fight—no opportunity to feel intensely alive. But was I merely projecting my own reflections onto this animal? Might it not have answered that it was perfectly happy on the sofa in front of the TV and had no desire or longing whatsoever for the snow, toil, and hunger of the mountains? I don't know, and we will probably never find out.

Nonetheless, I would rather rejoice in the knowledge that the wolverine exists out there in the wild than see it tame and cowering behind a fence.

I sometimes experience the same feeling about nature that is fenced in, if it's just a pitiful remnant of something that once existed, if I know there's a busy highway right behind this hill, and buildings behind that other one. I like nature when it's part of something bigger; when you can march for a day or more without encountering any roads or encroachments—which is the definition of the wilderness that now barely exists anymore, even in the wilderness land of Norway. The Norwegian Environment Agency defines nature with wilderness characteristics as lying at least five kilometers, or a little over three miles, from major encroachments on nature. Three miles—that's not exactly a day's march, and yet barely over 10 percent of Norway's land qualifies even as this. At the beginning of the twentieth century, half of the country still had wilderness characteristics, but the illusion that Norway is a land of nature where there's always plenty to go around has wiped out not just many of the country's wild animals but also most of the wilderness.

Chadwick betrays no disappointment over the fact that the wolverines have so easily set aside their wildness, allowing themselves to be tamed and even to be scratched under the chin. I'm a bit uncertain myself; if nothing else, this is another reason to wonder what can be going through the wolverine's head. It has honed its hunting skills and ingenuity in an inhospitable landscape over hundreds of thousands of years, and would never have survived if it had only a standard, narrow repertoire of instincts at its disposal. The wolverine has the ability to learn, a capacity for judgment, and ingenuity. Descartes's thesis that animals were automata is naturally wrong, but the notion still gained a foothold and has done irreparable damage by justifying a view of animals as something akin to objects. But they are curious, capable of learning, inventive, playful, and they may also have a certain feeling for the magnificent natural world of which they form a part. And while some of their actions are evil by our standards, there is no such thing as an evil animal.

AS WE STAND in front of the wildlife camera beside the den in Wolverine Valley and watch the recording of the wolverine that had stood beside the opening some days earlier, Espen speaks about his first encounter with the species, on a wildlife camera set up beside a different den. The wolverine didn't make a very good first impression. In the video, the female leaves the den, Espen tells us, and shortly afterward, a male sneaks inside, but it comes out almost immediately carrying a cub that it has bitten to death. Then it goes in and fetches a second cub. After that, it sits down right in front of the wildlife camera and eats both of them up before vanishing, apparently unmoved by this atrocity. After a while, the female returns and sees the tragedy. What does she feel? Bottomless grief, or a resigned realization that this is just the way wolverine life is? Tough and brutal. No one can know, but maybe she'll soon mate with the child murderer—which was the male's goal. The wolverine is not alone in this bestial behavior. Many larger predators do the same thing, and it can't be classed as evil—that requires a capacity for moral reflection—but rather as a strategy for fulfilling nature's sole imperative: to spread your genes. If the male succeeds in his attempt to seduce the female afterward, that is a result of the same strategy on her part.

It's impossible not to feel distaste for the male sex when those beautiful nature-porn programs the BBC specializes in follow polar bear or lion families in which the females not only birth and raise the cubs but also risk their lives hunting for food—*and* must simultaneously protect both food and cubs from the males. But while it's true that wolverines and nature aren't moral role models, we do also find examples of boundless love. These mothers will stop at nothing to defend their young while they are alive, although once they no longer are, there's little to be gained from a collapse into apathy and depression. Nature is also an arena for cooperation and acts of beauty.

Maybe those dead white swans on the newly frozen ice of the dark lake exemplified love and lifelong fidelity, whereas the wolverine might seem to be the opposite: a vicious child killer, all compact muscle and razor-sharp teeth; a killing machine with a bone-crunching bite, which will happily eat a horse, or at least a reindeer, skin and hair and all—versus a graceful, white, monogamous swan. We humans have this need for dichotomies, for black-and-white narratives, for good and evil, and we apply it to nature too. We distinguish between animals and beasts, and even though the moral awareness of the wolverine and swan is identical—both are *amoral*, neither is immoral—the wolverine undoubtedly has some peculiarities that bear out its mythology.

It often rips the head off its prey, and in forested areas it may scale a tree and deposit reindeer heads, even entire calves, high up in the branches. This almost inconceivable display of power certainly helps shore up the wolverine's legendary status. The fact that the animal weighs roughly thirty pounds and the reindeer perhaps ten times as much further bolsters the mythology. Sometimes, wolverines may also hang parts of their prey's carcass in surrounding trees, as if performing some voodoo ritual of the wilderness. Apparently, although it's hard to tell where folklore takes over from reality with this creature, the wolverine sometimes digs a hole beneath its prey so it can guard it after marking it with its most pungent secretions.

The wolverine is at the very top of the food chain and has no reason to fear any other animals. It is one of the few species that can count on dying at a ripe old age, so why do we never find dead wolverines? What becomes of them? The fact is that few wolverines die a natural death; the vast majority are killed by humans. But Eivind tells me that dead cubs aren't such an unusual sight; some are killed by adult males, while others die of unknown causes. They once found a dead wolverine farther into the mountains here, too; perhaps one of the very few to die a natural death, at an advanced age.

We drive back on rotting snow and across the spreading bare patches. A rough-legged buzzard glides above us, recognizable by its broad, eagle-like wings, white on the underside with a black patch. The snowmobiles are driven into the hangar. Eivind and Espen plan to head out next week too and promise to keep me updated about any new finds over the spring.

Down in Gudbrandsdalen it's just above freezing point on this April day. If I'm to have any hope of tracking wolverines again before the summer, I'm going to have to go even higher up, into Jotunheimen. I'm planning to cover part of the route of my first-ever proper mountain hike, my aimless ramble through the *real* mountains of Jotunheimen. On that trek, also nearly fifty years ago now, my friend Kjetil and I had only bivouac bags, homemade cooking utensils, and a 1938 map—although we made up for our inadequate equipment and lack of experience with the arrogance and sense of immortality of youth. We crossed endless bogs in Murudalen in the dark of night, were sent packing by dairymaids when we asked to stay overnight at a summer farm, and instead ended up cooking porridge with our rudimentary cookware before creeping into our bivouac bags and spending a wretched night out on the pastureland. After the milk truck woke us at the crack of dawn the next day, we pressed on through the lower part of the beautiful Sjodalen valley as the sun rose, hiked through increasingly sparse pine forest, and then endured a tough climb up scree slopes before reaching the peak of

Nautgardstind, our first time above 7,200 feet. As I stood up there, I thought to myself: this is what life will be like from now on—peaks and hikes. Little did I know! From Nautgardstind, which is an endless scree slope both up and down, we crossed the Veo River and hiked up to Trollsteinhøe, which has an almost Alpine pre-summit peak on its western approach, whereas the mountain itself is nothing but a heap of gravel despite its altitude of 7,221 feet. We felt that this first anonymous peak deserved a name of its own, though, and dubbed it Jervetind—Wolverine Peak! The name appeared out of nowhere, probably inspired by the overwhelming emotions that suddenly flooded me amid all these peaks and gorges, all this freedom and wilderness, which sparked associations with the wolverine. When we returned home from our hike, we wrote a naive, high-flown description of the trek for the local newspaper, paying homage to the peak. We even wrote a poem to it!

It really *was* relatively untrodden back then, and the name we gave it certainly made sense. This is a region where the wolverine roams. A couple of local girls had recently met one at a spot just "a stone's throw" from Jervetind (which is now officially known as Southern Trollsteinhøe, a much more prosaic name if you ask me). And it was a *real* meeting. The wolverine sauntered toward them, eventually getting so close (a distance of twenty yards or so) that the girls' pulse rates rocketed. Yet they still had the presence of mind to film the unusually beautiful specimen, with its golden-brown back, pale flanks, and dark belly. Although the wolverine must have been aware of the shrieking girls, it continued to approach them impassively until their screams became so loud that it swung calmly to the left and headed up into the scree slope. I've watched the short clip they posted online with considerable envy. There are stories of wolverines playing in the snow, oblivious to the folks nearby, so the animal isn't *always* all that shy, but it would never think of attacking people.

THIS AREA, near Jervetind, is where I'm thinking of going, but there's simply not enough snow, and certainly no snow firm enough to bear my weight, so I ski up onto the high mountain plateau of Valdresflye instead and strike out west along Leirungsdalen valley. There's still plenty of skiable snow here. I gradually veer northward, following the ridge up toward Høgdebrotet—a friendly peak despite its altitude of roughly 7,300 feet, which also has some fabulous traverses with poetic names like Razor Ridge, or the narrow passage over to Tjørnholstind, where my partner Hanne Line and I hiked three months after we nearly died in the storm, to convince ourselves we hadn't developed a fear of mountains.

It was on my first ascent of Høgdebrotet's gentle slope that I encountered something that would mark a watershed in our springtime cross-country treks into the mountains: climbing skins. One May, a couple of months after our lyrical christening of Jervetind, Kjetil and I found ourselves zigzagging up this long, slow incline, sweating away on waxed skis that barely had any grip. Halfway up, we were overtaken by three girls in shorts wearing backcountry skis who laughingly left us in the dust as they effortlessly ascended the slope. They had skins on their skis!

In this soggy snow on a sunny hillside my skins are my salvation today. I stop off on a bare heathery hillock, where I eat, then change into shorts and a short-sleeved shirt. On another bare patch just twenty yards away, a male ptarmigan sits and cackles, red-combed and bursting with life. I once came across a ptarmigan nest at the very base of Høgdebrotet's long east-facing ridge. Although the mother bird fluttered around the tips of my boots, it was a while before I spotted the five eggs. They lay between two distinctive rocks, so on my way back down, I sat up on the hillside with my binoculars planning to watch the mother ptarmigan on her nest. But even though I knew exactly where she was, I still failed to catch sight of either her or the nest again.

I like going uphill. Once you find your rhythm and get into the flow, it becomes effortless, and the climb creates a calm space in which to savor the spring sun on your back, breathe in the wonderful scent of heather on the hillocks, and notice that the snow buntings have come back to prepare for nesting season. I see the mountains around me, all familiar friends, and find myself reminiscing about various routes and traverses. There's still sun on top of Høgdebrotet but it's setting fast and a chill wind is picking up. It's almost impossible to convey the sensation of sitting on top of the mountain in absolute silence and gazing at the peaks around me without falling into cliché, much less to add anything original to the plethora of existing descriptions of precisely this sensation. Nor am I able to rationally explain my fascination for something that is not a prerequisite for human life and evolution. Stone, snow, steep cliffs, slog—sometimes cold, fear, and actual danger. The view toward Jotunheimen south of Lake Gjende as you ascend is always splendid too, a source of joy, anticipation, and yearning that is reminiscent of love. And hiking alone in the valleys, high up in the mountains, among the peaks on a sunny day like this gives me a feeling of happiness that lacks any rational basis. It isn't a sense of achievement—that's what you get after struggling your way to the top, although this can be enhanced by the feeling that there's a tiny element of risk involved. But a sense of achievement isn't enough to give me this feeling of happiness and harmony, of being at peace with myself that I get when I see the view from a peak. As a biologist, I'm always seeking out rational explanations for emotions, pleasures, and pains. Most of them are obvious, but some are not. Longing, nostalgia, and the joy you feel on a peak are among the inexplicable emotions, and it's perfectly fine that some things can't be classified in purely logical terms. These kinds of emotions have become more intense with age as I have realized with a certain melancholy that I no longer have an infinite number of such sunlit mountain hikes ahead of me.

From my vantage point on top of Høgdebrotet I sweep my binoculars back and forth across the mountainsides. Supposedly reliable sources claim that wolverines climb up to the summit in this precise spot, and sit here scanning the mountains and plateaus for reindeer, which, unbeknownst to them, bear the brand of the local *tamreinlag*—or the semi-domesticated reindeer herding district. But there are no wolverines here today—not that I'd expected there to be.

On my way up, I crossed what might have been a wolverine track, but the sun had already ruined it, so it was impossible to say for sure. I know that the wolverine is here someplace, that I *could* have seen it, and again I console myself by thinking that it's enough to know it's here, or *almost* enough.

As twilight advances, I glide down from the peak. The sun has softened the uppermost layer of snow, giving me perfect conditions for a smooth descent. Only by the time I'm down on the flat does the approaching night frost begin to form a crusty layer over the soft snow. Winter will linger for a long time up here and never quite loosens its grip. The snowdrifts will persist throughout the summer on the shady hillsides and river gorges, glaciers lie at the bottoms of the fjords, and sometimes it even snows up here in July. Still, spring has unmistakably arrived in the mountains, too, judging by the sweet scent of the heathery hillocks. According to a buddy who's even more obsessed with the joys of snow than I am, spring is the cross-country skiers' fall, but for me, spring is also the cross-country skiers' spring. However, it will be impossible to follow a physical wolverine track in the months ahead.

That afternoon, I pack my bag, shut up the cabin, head down the mountain in the magical twilight, and I arrive back in the city long after midnight. Although my mood always sinks like a barometer as I descend from mountain to lowland, especially when nature gives way to urban surroundings, an expectant light still lingers over the landscape.

Spring

If only we could hold on to those spring mornings of feverish birdsong in the half-light of dawn, when the forest smells of spring and the sunlight heralds one of the first warm days; the late May evenings with their dark-blue skies and intense scent of bird cherry; the nights, never entirely dark here in the north, filled with restlessness and inexplicable yearning; the sight of bright green fields burgeoning with yellow dandelions and the snow-clad peaks behind them; the feeling that the whole summer lies before you, intact. All those days and nights when you just have to be outside, in nature, a part of it. But the days run through our fingers like sand and then the spring is gone. The birdsong falls silent, having done its work. The song has won the singer territory and partners, and now what matters is rearing the next generation. The flowers stop blooming to embark upon their real job: producing seeds. Their colors and scents were nothing but a ploy to ensure propagation. The year's fervid youth is at an end; spring no longer surges. But the mountains offer a chance to prolong the spring. Up in the Ringebu Mountains, it lingers on into mid-June, and the leaves on the downy birches are not yet fully formed.

On June 12, I let myself into the cabin in the pale spring night. No one has been here since my last visit in winter. It's chilly in the mountains, and the foliage has taken on that peculiarly vivid green hue in the evening sun. A brambling *rheeee*s relentlessly beyond the cabin and the redwing's trills resound, but the place is otherwise surprisingly quiet. The old bird box in the birch is currently housing flycatchers, and six beautiful blue eggs lie in pairs on a nest of yellow straw. It's chilly inside the cabin too. I open the curtains, check whether the mice have found their way into the kitchen cabinet—they haven't—and open the trapdoor to the cellar to check the status down there. It's a storage space containing bottles of cordial, jam, tinned food, a few cans of beer, some bottles of soda. Most of its contents were stored here more than ten years ago and probably shouldn't be touched, although the jam is likely to be perfectly edible.

There may be no snow for tracking, but it's still possible to follow in the wolverine's footsteps even now. The female wolverine and her young have abandoned their den and are in urgent need of food. There's also still some hope of seeing their prints in the remaining snowdrifts that the reindeer seek out when warmer weather comes. There is a chance of encountering the wolverine's prey too. I weigh up two options for the next day's hike, both along rivers. Either the Breia or a considerably more inaccessible river valley farther north where I know lynxes live. I've only climbed down there once to check out the fishing prospects, and when I finally got to the bottom, I came across a skeleton. The head was missing, and my first thought was that some unlucky angler had ended his days at the bottom of the cliff, but then I realized it was a reindeer or a young moose. Few people would bother clambering down here—it's certainly not a great spot for fishing. The river has its modest origins in a large mountain lake, is then supplemented by expanses of bogland, and grows stronger as tributaries feed into it. There are taluses and steep slopes here, but no smooth reaches or pools to offer subsistence to fish. It was difficult to make any headway, but back then, several decades ago, I was sure that I would come back and follow the river upstream one day, out of the gorge, and into the mountains. Obviously, I was more likely to find good fishing out on the plateaus and closer to the mountain lake.

But I won't be following the course of a new river today. The weather is changeable, so I opt for the simplest solution: the Breia. I also mull taking a fly-fishing rod, but since it'll be a longish hike, I settle for a small telescopic rod that works well with both worms and spinners. Just above the cabin toward the east is a cliff that extends for about two-thirds of a mile. I walk southward along the top, with a view into the mountains all the way. At the base of the cliff, the birch forest slants downward, increasingly interspersed with spruce the farther down the valley it descends, all the way down to a bog. A crane nested here once. And one year, a beaver also took to the mountains and built its lodge along the little river that runs through the bog. I lie on my stomach at the very edge of the cliff's highest point and scan the bogland with my binoculars. There are no cranes to be seen, and no beavers either. Then again, it's a good many years since I last saw any, and tourist traffic has increased here in the intervening time. Otherwise, though, the mountains are teeming with life: the redwing leads the way, along with the chaffinch, and the willow warbler. This last species is Norway's most common and probably most anonymous bird: small, brownish gray, and shy. Its song is reminiscent of a chaffinch's, only warmer and more melodious, and for me its song is the sound of summer itself. It may still be spring in the mountains in the first half of June, but some of summer's melodies are already audible.

As the cliff gradually flattens out, I turn east, walk down the birch-clad hillside, and cross the bog and the stream. From here, I follow a track southward toward the Breia. From the bog, it's twenty minutes before I hear the roar of the waterfall. This is where the river starts out on a rougher stretch after its slow, gentle descent from its source, the Breitjønn tarns. Suddenly the river changes character, its broad, calm course altering to reveal a more dangerous face as the water forces its way through a gorge between sheer cliffs and down into a deep black pool. There are several such cascades and pools farther down before the Breia reins itself in for a while and returns to its previous broad course. Beside the next pool is the place where the ravens nest on a sheer rock face that plummets down to the river. I walk carefully along the gorge and, as I make my way over the edge, a raven takes off above the empty nest. It may be a young adult, since ravens start the season early. They already start to cobble together their nests in February and may roost as early as March. It's mid-June now.

Ravens are such impressive birds that it's hardly surprising Odin kept company with them. Even within the same animal group, there's always one species that has chosen a cognitive niche: the octopus among invertebrates, humans among mammals, and ravens among birds. Game birds have game-bird brains. But whereas a black grouse hen will always flee from danger, a full-grown turkey hen tends to attack any manageably sized individual that comes too close to her nest. When the turkey chicks hatch, she's the very model of a loving mother—as long as her hearing isn't impeded. But if she can't hear, she perceives her own chicks as intruders and pecks them to death. How can this happen? Doesn't she know her own offspring? Well, yes, but only from the sound they make. When she can no longer hear her chicks cheeping, the instinct to attack takes over. If a stuffed chick is pulled past a hearing mother on a string, it, too, will be greeted with angry pecks because she won't hear any cheeps from it either. But if you insert a loudspeaker into, say, a stuffed weasel and then pull it past the nest while playing a recording of a cheeping chick, there will be no attack.[19]

Ravens, by contrast, not only choose to build their nests on inaccessible shelves but also assess the situation carefully. Of course, there's no reason to make moral judgments about game birds, which have simply evolved different strategies than corvids, but we humans do have a tendency to rank other species according to their intelligence.

Farther down below the raven's nest the terrain becomes impassable, so I turn and go back to "my" pool, clamber down onto a flat rock that juts out over the water, and cast a hook baited with a worm up toward the waterfall. It's quite deep here, and a steady stream of bubbles rises from the black water, released after being dragged down into the depths. There's usually some trout here, all seemingly identical in size—just big enough to be what you might call a decent frying fish, no bigger. They probably made their way down from Breitjønn at some point and may have spent some time in smaller calm reaches farther upriver, but after this waterfall, there's no way back. Their only alternative is to carry on down, but since it's impossible to know what kind of waterfalls lie ahead, many choose to settle in this pool for the rest of their lives.

The fish here are always in good condition, which suggests that the river offers an ample supply of insects, but they never grow very big. At least none of the ones I've seen. So it's hardly surprising that they bite when a worm presents itself in their field of vision. Yet they're always cautious and you must always strike the moment you feel the first quiver on your line; otherwise, they'll neatly pick the worm clean without even touching the hook. Dad was a fly fisher and taught me the noble art. There's something special about this kind of angling, but narrow gorges where the thing you're most likely to hook is the scrub on the cliff behind you don't really lend themselves to it, which is why I haven't used my flies today.

I haven't fished here for many, many years, but I know exactly when and how hard to strike. I get a bite straight away on my first cast and catch two decent fish on my first two. Okay, so it isn't quite the kick I'd get from hooking a huge salmon, but even for a restless soul, there's a joyous sense of reunion and an uncommon calm to be had from standing on this familiar rock that juts out over the pool, casting my line those few yards under the waterfall, and then reeling it back in. Even though I know exactly what's on the other end of the line when I get a bite, actually landing it is still exciting. A half-pound fish is perfectly fine, and who knows—maybe one day, I'll hook a one-pounder. The fish here are all perfectly alike, their bellies a bright yellow to creamy yellow hue. The underlying color on their flanks and back is gray, although here, too, the creamy yellow shines through. The spots, or rather patches, are dark, but encircled by a paler ring. They begin directly below the lateral line, becoming larger and denser the farther up the back they are. At the rear, toward the tail fin, they are interspersed with red patches. An attractive fish in all respects, whose local name, *aur*, references the sand or gravel where it best likes to breed, because its spots offer excellent camouflage there.

The ubiquitous common sandpiper, Norway's most common wader, whistles its penetrating, jittery song, as it does beside so many rivers and lakes. Just beyond where I stand, here by the waterfall, it is briefly accompanied by a white-throated dipper, with its brown head, black back, and white underbelly. While the sandpiper turns aside at the waterfall, the dipper angles deftly upward and vanishes behind the cascading water, to the far right. This is where it has its nest and probably some chicks that will almost be flightworthy, since the white-throated dipper starts breeding almost as early as the raven. In the lowlands it may already be brooding as early as April, but up here it probably waits until May. Norway's national bird was long assumed to be as monogamous as the swan—and given its status, it ought to be a role model, of course—but closer investigation taught us otherwise.

In a large multiyear study that looked at an entire watercourse, we found that 10 percent of white-throated dipper males were involved with two females at any given time. One even had three partners. The same goes for the sandpiper, by the way, which also enjoyed the undeserved reputation of being strictly monogamous for a long time. The male dipper at least has the decency to stick around and help feed the chicks, so taking on two or even three broods involves considerable effort. It was long assumed that infidelity was the sole preserve of male birds, but that isn't true. The females' trick is to mate with the attractive handyman, while the possibly duller but faithful breadwinner provides food for the roosting female and then her chicks—probably blissfully unaware that they aren't his. The white-throated dipper is a bird that commands respect, hanging on through the winter, when it fearlessly dives into the channels between the ice in search of daily sustenance.

I'm not a patient angler, so after fifteen minutes without a bite, I switch to a shimmering silver spinner. Once more, it works on the first cast, but after that, it goes dead again. On the fifth cast, I let the spinner sink too deep and it snags between two rocks. There's no room for maneuver here, as I'm standing on the very edge of the projecting rock above the pool and can't go farther in any direction. The line breaks, but it's hardly a crisis. Three fish will do, and besides I'm planning to hike far and wide across the mountains today.

Like anyone else who ever read Helge Ingstad's *Land of Feast and Famine* in their youth and dreamed of a life beneath the open skies, I've done a great deal of thinking about how I would survive living only off the bounty of nature. The book is Ingstad's account of his adventures in Northern Canada in the 1920s, partly on his own, partly with Indigenous peoples. There and then, nature yielded decent meals via hunting and fishing.

With considerable effort, I might be able to keep myself going for a while in the Norwegian mountains with my fishing rod. A bit longer with an otter board. A shotgun would supplement my diet nicely, while a 30mm mesh net would provide more than enough fish with a minimum of effort, even under the ice. But it's an illusion to think you could survive long term in the mountains living only off the food nature has to offer, or at least do so without resorting to poaching fish and game, especially if many other people chose to live out the same wilderness dream as you. Still, there's a satisfaction to be had from eating self-picked blueberries instead of the imported variety in a plastic tub, or trout from a river rather than salmon from a pen.

After gutting the fish, I take a turn around the waterfall, registering as I do a track and a campfire site precisely where I'd have located it myself—on a broad shelf above the rapids, sheltered by the rock face with a nice view of the river. A beautiful spot. There's never anything accidental about the location of a campfire site. Others have discovered this idyll before me and have sat here frying their trout on a summer evening. But I'm hiking onward today. It makes sense to follow the Breia into the mountains, but the first part of the hike is a mixed bag: although it takes me through dense forest, it is still almost free of mosquitoes and flies so early in the year. At midsummer, they are the scourge of this birch forest and one of the reasons why I usually head up into the highlands at that time of year.

After a few hundred yards, I turn off onto the track that leads to Breistølen, and that's when I spot it. A canid slinks out of the birch forest and crosses my path no more than a hundred yards ahead of me. Something about its appearance makes me freeze: calm, almost self-assured, it strides across the agricultural road before vanishing into the forest on the other side. It was remarkably large and long-legged for a fox, wasn't it? And wasn't it gray? No. I've seen my fair share of foxes and this wasn't one of them. I can rule out dogs because there are no people up here. Then it strikes me that it must have been a wolf, that I have just had my first sighting of a *wolf* in the wild. It wouldn't be such a long trek from the wolf zone east of here for a young male roaming around in search of its own home range. Here I am, with the wolverine as my mental companion, and the animal that appears is the wolf! But how certain can I be? Is 80 percent certain enough, 95 percent?

I conclude to myself that it may not matter all that much. Highly likely is good enough for me. The mere knowledge that wolves exist in these mountains is sufficient to give me this sense of intactness, wildness, grandeur. The areas between the valleys of Gudbrandsdalen and Østerdalen retain elements of the original ecosystem that evolved after the Ice Age, with reindeer and the big four: wolverines, bears, wolves, and lynxes. Although the predator populations are kept at the viable minimum, they do at least exist. And now I have seen a wolf in the wild. I hurry to the spot where it crossed the road, but of course it has vanished altogether, leaving behind it only a sense of unreality. There isn't even any damp soil on the edge of the trail that could reveal tracks. Although I know it's pointless, I stand on the edge of the road for a long while, hoping that it might come into view again.

It's still early in the morning when I reach Breistølen and hike up toward Øverlihøgda. Where I battled through snow three months ago, I now struggle through a wilderness of willow thickets. No one could claim nature is all sunshine and rainbows. Biting insects and flies hardly enhance a mountain hike, and willow thickets aren't a favorite either, but these wetland areas are among the most productive in the mountains. And I really ought to put in a good word for mosquitoes, too—or rather Nematocera, the suborder to which they belong. Although I loathe bloodsucking mosquitoes as much as the next person, there's more to Nematocera than this much-hated member, not least midges, of which Norway has at least five hundred species, versus just thirty-eight types of mosquito; and midges are the Nematocera of the highlands par excellence. Their larvae mostly live in water, and on still days when mass hatching is underway, you can hear buzzing clouds of insects as they dance over the willow thicket, fulfilling the biological imperative of passing on their genes. Just as dragonflies, stone flies, caddis flies, mayflies, and others do when the time has come for hatching and the courtship dance. These short, hectic days of dalliance in the mountains give life not just to new generations of insects but also to new generations of birds, fish, and—directly or indirectly—a lot of other highland wildlife.

What has happened to insects over these five decades? Well, the number of flies, mosquitoes, midges, and gnats may have remained stable here in the mountains where the lakes and bogs and birch forests are still intact. Populations here are probably driven by summertime rainfall and temperatures, although no one knows for sure. Yet globally, insect numbers seem to be dwindling, and that doesn't just apply to the charismatic pollinators but to bugs in general. Nature has shrunk over these same years, and monocultural farming, the spread of asphalt, ditching, drainage, and pesticides have all taken a toll on the winged masses, including birds. Fewer insects mean less food and fewer birds, at a time when birds are already suffering from shrinking nature and an increasing human population. Norway is no exception: here, too, there are fewer birds—that is, fewer individuals of many species. We are falling victim to shifting baselines. I have only the vaguest grasp of the population density of insects and birds fifty years back, and when old folk claim that there is less birdsong, that *could* just be a result of hearing loss—if it weren't for the fact that we have long time series recording migration and hatching that reflect this very decline.

That said, wolverine and reindeer numbers have actually risen here in the mountains over the same half century, although only because both species had been hunted to minimal levels fifty years ago. If we were to set our reference point one or two hundred years before *that*, the situation would look quite different. Reindeer hunting is now more strictly regulated, but the species is under pressure from the inexorable rise in the number of people keen to hike or own cabins in the reindeer's realm. In other mountain regions, they are regularly shot in an attempt to wipe out chronic wasting disease. Some think that the wolverine is what's needed to keep the disease in check. After all, the wolverine is the mountain's busboy, specializing in clearing away dead, injured, or sick animals.

I follow an old trail east into the mountains. The path follows the only passable route here, along a river that runs parallel to the Breia, but farther south. On the north side of the path lie bogs and wetlands, on the southern side, across the stream, impenetrable willow thickets and birch forest. But the path follows a dry, open route along a steep hill down toward the stream. Somewhere down there in the willow, the bluethroat sings a melodious phrase that starts with the chime of a silver bell. I fail to spot it, which is a shame because, with its red and blue breast, it's the jewel of the willow thicket. At some point in their evolution, the robin redbreast and the bluethroat parted ways. The bluethroat ended up with a blue breast that surrounds a rust-red patch, then a black band that borders a larger red patch below. The robin is also a master singer but produces a quite different soundscape. The nightingale is a member of their family too, but melodious birdsong is not necessarily a marker of the clan—think of thrushes, for example.

The fieldfare is a ubiquitous noisy presence here in the birch forest, but why can't I find any thrush nests nowadays? I, who found them everywhere in my boyhood and climbed up to countless nests in the spring to see the fieldfares' greenish, brown-speckled eggs. The answer is threefold, the first and most important factor being time. Back then I had plenty of time, and used to go out into nature to experience it. The second is that I was, so to speak, programmed to find birds' nests. Dad always wondered how I could spot them, but the fact is that my radar was set to detect them. The third, more prosaic explanation is, perhaps, that my eyesight is poorer. But the fieldfare loudly announces that it has a nest in the vicinity, and this alert is what eventually helps me to spy a nest today, high up in a slender birch. That's enough to satisfy me. A bit later, I come across a nest at head height, and while it is empty, from last year, this year's nest is close by: high up but in a solid tree, so I quickly shin up it. Climbing is a skill that is deeply rooted in us humans, and until recently in our history, it could still save your life in an encounter with a predator. I can't count how many trees I climbed as a boy to visit nests. Always quickly up and quickly down, to cause as little disturbance as possible, but up I *had* to go. Even to the rough-legged buzzard's nest up on the rock face, even to the crow's nest at the top of the highest spruce in the neighborhood, yes, even to the tawny owl's nest in a big bird box. The tawny owl was not to be messed with, and it attacked silently. A friend of mine lost an eye as a result of its assault, and I myself came away with blood pouring from my neck.

Over time, new interests took over, and busyness. After my teenage years, I never climbed trees again and unlearned not just the joy of bird's-nest aesthetics but also the habit of spending time in nature, and perhaps even the ability to *immerse* myself and simply be present in nature. Now, though, I note with satisfaction that both my tree-climbing skills and my enjoyment of this activity are undimmed. As I haul myself up to the edge of the nest, I also take pleasure in seeing the fieldfare's familiar eggs once again. It's early in the nesting season, and so far there are only three.

Willow undergrowth is manageable as long as it's dry, but wet, three-foot-high willow thickets are a real ordeal. The damp of last night's dew still lingers but the sun is starting to break through, and once I've gotten past the willow and into the sparse birch forest above, the weather is fine. From here, I follow the easily walkable ridge that leads into the mountains parallel to the river, in the direction of the plane wreck. When I catch sight of Storkvien, the highest peak in this area, I turn south toward the wolverine talus. On my way, I pass an intact trapping pit that I remember seeing before. It's roughly five feet deep, maybe six feet long, and about three feet wide, and is lined with sheer, perfectly built stone walls. With leading fences and sharp poles in the bottom, it would still be capable of trapping reindeer maybe a thousand years after a group of trappers managed to dig deep down into the hard, stony ground, then picked out rough stones with at least one flat surface, laboriously built walls, and thus created a grave that would last millennia. Reindeer may have roamed this area for as long as eight thousand years, and the wolverine for almost as long; humans came later. So while both have competed for reindeer here for millennia, the wolverine came first.

I've studied the map since I was here last, and now I think I know where the talus must be, the one I didn't find again in winter. I zigzag through the terrain, beneath all the cliffs and outcrops, until, at last, I find a rough talus beneath a small crag, higher up the mountainside than I remembered. I find the femur of a small reindeer, but it's impossible to tell if a wolverine brought it here. I find no other signs that any wolverines have been in the vicinity: no pungent odor from the opening between two large rocks that must be the way down into a den—if there is one.

For many years, wolverines were essentially absent from these mountains, and it wasn't until the late 1970s that they made their way back to the areas around Rondane and bred there. When it comes to the location of wolverine litters, a razor-sharp boundary runs across Norway at a slight slant: to the east, down toward the Swedish border in central Norway, and to the west, toward the fjords, but wolverines steer clear of the central Norwegian coast. The place where I am now is just inside this boundary, but if any wolverines have bred their young in this talus in modern times, that would make it one of the southernmost outposts. Otherwise, the wolverine is possibly the most typically boreal of all predators. It is distributed along the conifer belt around the entire northern hemisphere; the whole of Siberia, and most of the northern conifer forests of the United States and Canada. It is an animal more of the forests than the mountains and was once even more widespread—living as far afield as Thoreau's gentle forests outside Concord, Massachusetts, northwest of Boston. Thoreau describes the loss of the wolverine in these forest regions in a way that anticipates the words of E. O. Wilson and other writers over a century later:

> But when I consider that the nobler animals have been exterminated here, the cougar, panther, lynx, wolverene, wolf, bear, moose, deer, beaver, turkey, etc., etc.—I cannot but feel as if I lived in a tamed, and, as it were, emasculated country... As if I were to study a tribe of Indians that had lost all its warriors... I take infinite pains to know all the phenomena of the spring, for instance, thinking that I have here the entire poem, and then, to my chagrin, I learn that it is but an imperfect copy that I possess and have read, that my ancestors have torn out many of the first leaves and grandest passages, and mutilated it in many places. I should not like to think that some demigod had come before me and picked out some of the best of the stars. I wish to know an entire heaven and an entire earth.[20]

A solitary wanderer like Thoreau probably felt a sense of kinship with the wolverine, which also roams from horizon to horizon. Truth to tell, I feel that kinship myself, whenever I feel the peace of mind that only comes from heading for the next blue ridge, free of limits, interruptions, or chitchat. And I imagine that the wolverine, too, the wild wolverine, would agree that weather, wind, cliffs, and ordeals are a crucial part of really experiencing life.

The wolverine has many remarkable physiological traits that enable it to live its life under extreme conditions, including an ability to breed with precision. After mating, which may take place between April and August, the female can assess the situation and "choose" to delay the implantation of the fertilized egg in the wall of the uterus; in this way, she can postpone fetal development until conditions seem more propitious. After that, it takes just one to one-and-a-half months—a remarkably short gestation for such a large animal—for the two or three cubs to be born, sometime in midwinter, or March at latest. By fall, they must be self-sufficient; no mercy. Incidentally, one of the astonishing things about the dark-brown, sometimes almost black wolverine is that the newborn kits are white—like miniature polar bear cubs.

But despite their strength, their shyness, and their aura of the wilderness, wolverines live entirely on terms set by humans. We have full control. A paragraph in Norway's wildlife management regulations sets an annual ceiling of thirty-nine wolverine litters per year. So what happens to surplus litters? Some are "taken out" during the breeding season: the female is shot near its den, which is then excavated and the kits are exterminated after a life so short they never even got to see the light of day. It's hard to imagine a nastier system for managing a threatened species, especially given Norway's special duty of stewardship as home to more than a quarter of Europe's wolverine population. Both the wolverines and those tasked with carrying out the ghastly deed have my profoundest sympathy.

LAST WINTER, I flew down to Borkebua cabin on skis with the wind at my back; now it's a tough hike on foot, but the day is windless, and though the sun is low, it's still warm. Once there, I take out a prepackaged mini-ration of butter, cream, salt, and pepper—I allowed myself that much confidence in my fishing skills. Using the camping stove and pan I've brought along with me, I fry the three trout in butter on a high flame to crisp the skin, then sit outside by the sunny wall and eat them accompanied only by salt, pepper, and cream. It's simply one of the best meals I know. Then I take out my binoculars. It's silent but for the faint babble of birdsong down toward Imsdalen, and I can hear the redwing in the birch forest. Fieldfare, of course, are here too. The bluethroat, the meadow pipit, and the reed bunting's unassuming, repetitive trill dominate from the watercourse below the cabin. The sound of the golden plover reaches me from the dry barrens, and once I hear the rough-legged buzzard's plaintive cry, though I cannot see it. Nor do I see any reindeer or, naturally, any wolverines. But as the sun sets and I'm about to go indoors, I catch a glimpse of a red fox down there beside the stream where I went to fetch water and throw away the remains of my trout supper. This one, at least, was indisputably a fox, and the contrast with the animal that crossed the agricultural road was palpable.

I've planned to spend the night at Borkebua, so I roll my sleeping bag out on the lower bunk, switch on my headlamp, and leaf through yet another book, this one entitled simply *The Wolverine Book*. The author, journalist Egil Hyldmo, has packaged up facts, stories, ancient sagas, and photographs into a small book as multifaceted and compact as the wolverine itself. I'm constantly learning new things about this animal, even though I was sure I already knew almost everything about it. Through tales and sagas, the book expands upon the wolverine's bad reputation as "a whirling, hairy mass, with glowing teeth and eyes, and searing, evil-smelling breath,"[21] but like everyone who has taken the trouble to look beyond the rumors, Hyldmo shows a deep warmth and respect for the persecuted and hated animal, and he has included some moving tales of wolverine hunts and kits abandoned in the den. The only thing worse than killing a litter in the den. I go and stand out on the flagstones in the pale night. This is one of the most hectic days and nights in the late spring mountains, and nature has no time to spare for sleep. There are still birds everywhere: I hear a rock ptarmigan on the hillside behind the cabin, and a fox barks deep down in the birch forest. Like the wildlife around me, I feel no compulsion to go to bed, and I slightly regret that I didn't bring along a hammock, so I wouldn't have to shut the door on this spring night.

THE NEXT MORNING, I hike over Gråhøgda, the mountain that shelters Borkebua from the north wind. It is a barren region, this, with little rainfall, and the soil is poor in lime, suitable only for the most unassuming of mountain flora that is capable of eking a slow, stunted life from the scant soil—and of withstanding wind, cold, and six or seven months beneath the snow besides. In the hollows, an occasional stunted juniper clings onto existence along with crowberry, a few grass species, and the odd cluster of moss campion, but other than this there are barely any flowering plants here. Mountain avens, which climbs up to 7,200 feet in Jotunheimen, is not a species that grows here, and neither will you find meadow anemone, golden root aka *Rhodiola rosea*, or any of the other most attractive highland plant species. Nor are there any of those perennial meadows of wolfsbane that you see in other mountainous regions blessed with higher rainfall and more lime-rich soil. This is the desert of the mountains, and moss is what makes these areas almost winter white in places: star-tipped cup lichen, green reindeer lichen, crinkled snow lichen, and the most unassuming of them all, map lichen, which transforms the gray rock talus into a marbled artwork in shades of yellow and green framed by a black border.

It isn't far from this spot that Dad and I found a gravestone for my sister Marit after searching long and hard. A solid, rectangular stone, smoothly rounded on top but with otherwise straight sides, and intricately decorated with map lichen. It was a huge effort to get that rock down to the road, but in all our grief over our pointless loss, it did us good to struggle with a hefty, tangible gravestone. And the map lichen on the stone is still holding out more than forty years later. Back then, I thought we were doing this for Marit, but all the beautiful gravestones, flowers on the grave, and other rituals to honor the memory of the dead are necessarily for our own benefit, for our own sake, and in some cases to assuage our sense of guilt.

There's a faint breeze from the north, so I find a small south-facing rock face where I plan to sit and scan the landscape with my binoculars once more. Of course, I don't expect to see a wolverine, but sitting calmly for a while with a pair of binoculars is the best way to observe life in the mountains. The reindeer are probably farther north now, but it's still worth looking out for them. As I'm about to sit down, a small, grayish-brown meadow pipit steals up between my feet. I know its nest must be on this hillock within a radius of less than two feet at most, but there's no guarantee I'll find it. I don't want to scare the little bird unnecessarily, either, but as it happens, it isn't long before I spot the brood chamber with six eggs low down on the hillock, surrounded by star-tipped cup lichen and under a dwarf birch twig. It's like a fieldfare's nest in miniature, made of the same building material, dry grass, and the eggs are also grayish green and speckled brown.

I hurry a few hundred yards farther before sitting down again. The first thing my binoculars alight on is the antlers of a big reindeer buck sticking up from the ground directly below me. After wandering down, I see there's actually a whole buck here, or its skeleton at least. It has been picked almost clean, although some tendons remain intact, and it is lying on a blanket of its own hide. When did it die? And why? It has chosen an impressive final resting place—if, that is, it got to choose: on the western flank of Gråhøgda, with South Breitjønn tarn below, surrounded by bogs, plateaus, and gentle peaks. To the northwest lie the great peaks of Rondane, still amply decked in snow, and the lighting is dramatic. Patches of sun here and there amid black clouds, and a veil of rain on the horizon, forming a gray link between heaven and earth.

The buck probably didn't draw its dying breath last winter, when I was skiing a bit farther east of here, but more likely in late summer or early fall. I peer directly toward the crag where the wolverine talus is located, but there's no reason to suspect the wolverine, unless this reindeer was injured or sick, had a broken bone, maybe, or—heaven forbid—chronic wasting disease. Did it have time to gaze out across its realm, aware that life was now over? If so, did it feel any kind of fear, not to say existential angst in the face of the unknown and the thought that it would never again be at one with nature in its kingdom, feel the spark of life, or mount a doe? I don't believe it felt any fear, unless a predator was hot on its heels. And even then, wild deer appear to resign themselves rapidly to such situations once they have been caught, as if they realize matter-of-factly that it's just the way life is.

Over time, we have accumulated an inconceivable body of knowledge about nature, about the evolution of animals, their ecology, and indeed about the innermost essence of their life in the form of metabolism and genes. But animals' thoughts will always elude us. There is something both fascinating and profoundly disquieting about the fact that we will never know about their inner life—if they even have one. But we can imagine, in principle, that mammals at least feel emotions in a similar way as we do. Animals like reindeer and wolverines undoubtedly experience some kind of joy; what would motivate them otherwise? Similarly, animals experience fear as a motivation to escape from its cause. We are bound to believe that animals like elephants, dolphins, and chimpanzees have a rich and advanced emotional register. But they are hardly likely to experience metaphysical yearnings, fear of the unknown, or the ability to ponder past, future, eternity, and the cosmos. And that means they have no need for any comforting fictions about gods, meaning, or eternal life either. Longing, nostalgia, and melancholy are probably uniquely human emotions, and it's hard to identify a rational basis for them either, other than that they are linked to an awareness of transience. Lost childhood, lost youth, a life that is ending forever. The death of a young person is almost unbearable for the bereaved. Animals, meanwhile, may grieve over their dead offspring for a time, but then life goes on. What do we know, though—elephants may grieve for decades. Will this reindeer buck be missed or remembered by the others? I don't think so, but I can't know. Nor do I think that it could feel that melancholy emotion I sometimes notice mingling with my experience of spring. When we see a blossoming bird cherry beneath a deep blue evening sky in May, even the anticipation of those bursts of happiness we'll get from walking barefoot on the beach on a summer's day is mingled with a melancholy that stems from our awareness that they are just that: bursts. Fall is on the way, and I must acknowledge that ever fewer such days remain to me. One day, this landscape will be here but my senses will no longer be able to take it in. I have slowly learned to accept this realization, and have found that it is bearable as long as I can count on others still being here and feeling, and as long as wolverines and reindeer continue to live here. I would be surprised to find that thoughts of this kind ran through the head beneath the reindeer's antlers in its final hour, but we shall never know.

We humans have long regarded ourselves as fundamentally different from animals; we have emphasized the uniquely human and often downplayed similarities and kinship. If we go a really long way back, to the time when we were in thrall to nature, we must believe that we saw ourselves as one species among many, without any notion of being God's chosen ones. Yet there are still some essential differences. We are probably the only species able to feel *existential pain*, although all animals respond to positive and negative stimuli in their environment, and "choose" what most benefits the advance of their family: eating without being eaten oneself, driven by the ultimate biological imperative of passing on one's own genes to the maximum possible extent. This is the common trait shared by all living things, and the key question is not *whether* humans are subject to this same imperative—we simply are—but *the extent* to which we are. Language, the capacity for abstraction, culture, and morality are human characteristics, but the only *fundamental* difference between humans and animals (and it is far from trivial, of course) is that animals lack the capacity for ethical judgment and *normative* morality. Nor is the difference here necessarily so great, in part because we ourselves only observe this normative morality to a limited extent, and even altruistic actions probably contain a significant element of self-interest. Moreover, our normative morality stems from the same mutuality and empathy we find among social animals.

To what extent do species, or does nature per se, possess a value that is detached from human judgment? One common argument is that "the value" of an organism is linked to *its capacity to suffer*, and it has been proven beyond a shadow of a doubt that animals can suffer—even though, as I've said, I have no idea whether a wolverine behind a fence feels sorrow or loss. It has commonly been assumed that moral virtues are not "natural," which means that a strong bulwark of ethical principles must stem from somewhere other than nature. This builds upon a misanthropic view that our "true nature" is dominated by morally negative traits such as aggression and egoism. Nature is cruelty, blood, violence, and the survival of the fittest; Alfred, Lord Tennyson's famous phrase "Nature, red in tooth and claw," from his elegy *In Memoriam A. H. H.* (1850), also inspired Charles Darwin. The wolverine is bloodthirsty, there's no doubt about that, but even if we perceive it as an incarnation of this description of nature, it is more than just a killing machine. Nature is also full of cooperation, and the capacity for empathy and collective solutions is prominent among social animals like ourselves. We could not have functioned as social individuals without qualities such as empathy any more than the other social primates. What's more, we have the capacity for ethical reflections about right and wrong behavior toward others. And these others need not only be our fellow humans, but also reindeer, wolverines, and all the rest of the life on our planet.

I abandon the skeleton of the great buck and continue northward along Gråhøgda's gentle western slope. On the northwestern side of the mountain there are three oases in this desert of stone and arid plateaus: the South, Inner, and North Breitjønn tarns, surrounded by reeds and bogland teeming with life. I descend to the smallest, the innermost tarn, where I saw that dead swan pair. The midges have already begun to swarm in the willow thicket, with the buzzing of billions of mosquitoes. A few redwings and northern wheatears clearly have their nests here, where the food is plentiful. But no bluethroats, which tend to live along the outlet stream. Life here is concentrated around these streams, the mountain's blood vessels. I lie down on a dry grassy patch by the stream, and it isn't long before I spot a stone fly nymph creeping along the bed, then another—and another still.

Stone flies are among the characteristic species you'll find in mountain streams. They belong to the group of evolutionarily ancient insects of the type that do not undergo full metamorphosis, unlike more "modern" insects, like beetles, butterflies, mosquitoes, flies, ants, wasps, bees, and others, which all start life as larvae. This stage is totally different from the adult form. In the larval stage, these insects live only to eat, eventually pupate, then break down into a cellular soup inside the pupa, only to rise again like the phoenix in a totally new guise. It's almost a miracle. Stone flies, however, spend their childhood and youth as nymphs, unfinished forms of their adult selves; here in the stream, they have flattened bodies, powerful clawed feet, and two cerci, or tail threads. When the nymphs reach maturity (assuming that they avoid being eaten by fish or white-throated dippers), they climb up onto a stone or straw, cast off one last skin, pump up their wings, and swarm upriver in clumsy flight for a few hectic days to lay their eggs and then die. As long as they manage to mate and the females manage to pass on the baton to the next generation in the stream, it makes no difference whether they die of old age after a few days or end up in the belly of a bluethroat. Mayflies' adulthood is even shorter, and neither they nor stone flies consume any nutrients as adults. Their entire youth is spent waiting for death, with mating as a brief if crucial intermezzo. For mayflies, reproduction is the sole and entire meaning of life.

You'll find the occasional caddis fly in the stream too. Unlike mayflies and stone flies—which, like them, are not really flies—caddis flies are modern insects that undergo complete metamorphosis. The larvae crawl around in a house they have fashioned from tiny stones, but other than that, their lives and fate resemble those of the other two: they swarm, they mate, and they die, to the delight of fish and birds. Some succeed in laying eggs before their day is done and so the cycle starts again, repeating itself as it has done for hundreds of thousands, indeed millions of years. Why? Neither they nor anyone else can answer that. Some *whys* don't have a *because*.

I hike up to the lake itself and peer down at the bed between the sparse reeds. Here too there are caddis flies, but these ones have built their houses from small scraps of reed or leaf because there's no chance of being swept away by the current here, so they don't need to haul around a heavy stone house. The northern phalarope can gorge on caddis flies here, but where on earth is it? This is the bird I'm keenest to see, and I know several pairs used to nest here. During my previous visit, a few years back, I spotted only a single pair, unintentionally flushing the well-camouflaged gray-brown male from its nest while its brightly plumaged partner paddled out on the lake. This year there seem to be none.

This swimming wader is one of the many examples of the unfathomable ways of evolution. In this case, it is the male who roosts on the nest and cares for the chicks, which is why he has gray-brown camouflage, whereas the female is a vividly colored beauty who generally abandons her partner and eggs long before she's set eyes on her ducklings. When a female is camouflaged, it seems natural to us, because she's the one who roosts and has to blend into the background; but strictly speaking, there's no reason the male shouldn't take on the nurturing duties, as in the case of the northern phalarope. In many bird species the male and female take turns roosting, but it's so rare to see the roles completely switched that we can't help wondering what triggered the transition. They probably used to brood in turn, but at some point in history, it proved more beneficial for the male to take over the role entirely. If a stay-at-home father resulted in more viable chicks than with the more common division of gender roles, evolution's job was simply to get on with refining this success. Assuming that the strong paternal instinct was heritable to some degree, the snowball would simply keep rolling, resulting in a new situation where only the male brooded and shed its beautiful coloring in keeping with its role change. The fact that the birds have had time to adapt their plumage suggests that this must be ancient history. But why haven't other waders followed suit?

Well, there *is* another species here in the mountains that has done so. A species known only to the initiated, the Eurasian dotterel: a beautiful wader with a white eye stripe, a brown back, and a glorious orange belly. Not to mention an astonishingly trusting nature. You can actually stroke its back when it's sitting on the nest, although it's best not to. Once the eggs are laid and the male is roosting, the female moves on and starts a new brood with another male.

From the female's point of view, this is rational: more offspring and less work; but it seems astonishing that the male would accept this. Surely he can't be so altruistic or *so* thoroughly naive. Yet we take it for granted that a female would accept a similar situation. Setting aside moral concerns, it simply boils down to evolution finding the strategy that results in the most viable offspring, even though that won't always be equally beneficial for both sexes. A balanced nuclear family model in which both partners contribute strikes us as "right" from the point of view of fairness; we have an intrinsic aversion to promiscuous freeloaders. But, like life, nature isn't always fair.

I trawl the bogs with my binoculars, scanning the reedbeds at the edge and the open stretches of water in search of these beautiful waders, which bob their heads as they swim; but they have disappeared. Maybe for good, or maybe they'll come back. The northern phalarope is, at any rate, classified as "near threatened," and thus one statistic among the many that speak of the decline in global biodiversity. I hike up the mountainside north of the lake to take one last overview, and a Lapland longspur shoots out of its nest right by the tips of my shoes. I note its characteristic grayish eggs with their dark speckles, flourishes, and decorations, but hurry onward. You don't bother a species that's categorized as "seriously threatened" without good reason. From above, I see the female flying low between the bushes before stealing over to the nest. If, as we biologists generally do, you are seeking rational reasons for shapes, colors, and everything else in nature, you might see the Lapland longspur's intricately ornamented eggs as a cast-iron insurance policy against the cuckoo's nest parasitism. Every Lapland longspur female lays eggs with their own specific coloring, a fingerprint the cuckoo can hardly hope to imitate; the Lapland longspur at least is safe from its freeloading ways.

The same can't be said of the meadow pipit, the cuckoo's favorite host. Its eggs display little imagination, so a cuckoo specializing in the meadow pipit has plenty of nests to choose from. In compensation, the meadow pipit has evolved a strong sense of suspicion and the ability to detect even tiny aberrations in size and color, which helps the mother bird oust a cuckoo egg before the cuckoo chick has a chance to do the same with *her* eggs. Meanwhile, the cuckoo has worked tirelessly over the generations to perfect its forgeries. The meadow pipit and the cuckoo are therefore locked into that race we see between all hosts and parasites. Our immune system learns to recognize protein structures on the surface of bacteria and viruses, which, in turn, respond by producing more sophisticated weapons driven by constant mutations. However, bird species that are more sporadic hosts can be incredibly naive, accepting cuckoos' eggs as their own even when they are completely different in size and color.

Another race is underway here: the constantly warming climate in the north is causing meadow pipits to bring forward their spring migration and breeding season. As short-distance migrants they respond more rapidly to an earlier spring than the cuckoo, which often spends the winter in Africa. Consequently, the cuckoo risks simply arriving too late to freeload off the meadow pipit, a situation the meadow pipit would hardly object to. Perhaps this may encourage it to bring forward its migration even more, since stragglers will bear the brunt of playing unwilling host to the cuckoo, whereas earlier migrators will benefit—unless they leave too early, of course. I can't say whether that's the reason the cuckoo is struggling too, but I have only heard its characteristic *cuck-oo* once, and only at a distance.

Despite being classified as "near threatened," though, the cuckoo and the meadow pipit will continue to have dealings with each other for the foreseeable future. Even though the European meadow pipit population has shrunk, the species is not endangered in Norway, where it is classified as of "least concern," with several million breeding individuals. Meanwhile the charismatic Lapland longspur population hasn't benefited from its creative egg designs: it has declined so dramatically over such a long period that there is genuine cause for concern. But nature is notoriously changeable. Concepts like "the balance of nature" lead many to think of nature as stable, but it most definitely is not; it's actually full of ups and downs—although mostly downs over the fifty years that have passed since I was first in this neck of the woods.

From the southern mountainside, I sweep my binoculars past the lake again and along the western flank of Gråhøgda, where I found the buck's skeleton, then onward to the distant areas where the wolverine talus lies. I don't expect to see any wolverines, but how about some reindeer? The second note on the first page of my *Zoo Journal* that opened with the wolverine track in 1972 reads as follows: "Heard corncrake several times on the field opposite Naustberget. Hessa." No words wasted there, but I was clearly aware that the corncrake was becoming a rarity. By as early as the 1950s it had more or less vanished from eastern Norway, although some were holding out in the west. It had always been one of the characteristic nocturnal sounds of summer in the hay fields below my father's childhood farm on the west-coast island. I'd heard it during the summer holidays of my own childhood in Western Norway. For a long time, the sound was a mystery to me. Little did I know then that it was produced by a species with the onomatopoeic Latin name of *Crex crex*. No matter how quietly we crept toward the spot where it was *crex*-ing away in the high grass, it inevitably vanished the moment the grass was pushed aside. I never saw the actual bird.

The efficiency gains of agriculture were bad news for the corncrake, whose populations rapidly declined once combine harvesters and mowing machines began to trim the fields and meadows. By 2008, there were only twelve corncrakes registered in this county of Western Norway, and there are estimated to be fewer than twenty-five breeding pairs in the entire country. From my lofty vantage point I ask myself what it would have been like to sit here in 1922, 1822, or 1722. I believe the mountains would have more to offer the farther back you went through these three centuries, precisely the era during which we have seriously subjugated nature.

That said, some species have thrived. On the cliff behind me is a noisy pair of ring ouzels, which make it abundantly clear that my presence is unacceptable so close to their nesting spot. Like the fieldfare, the ring ouzel has the strange habit of loudly announcing that it has a nest in the vicinity. If it kept quiet, the chances of finding the nest would be minimal. The fieldfare has a different strategy: a collective protection mechanism. The species often breeds in colonies, where it's all for one and one for all—so there's good reason to make a noise about the colony's existence. Most species avoid the fieldfares' defensive dive-bombing. The ring ouzel, on the other hand, has little to gain from broadcasting the location of its nest, but it does so all the same. Few people are familiar with this member of the thrush family, which resembles a blackbird, with the addition of a striking, crescent-shaped white neckerchief. My binoculars also pick up a pair of rough-legged buzzards circling overhead; once severely threatened, this species is now on the road to recovery. Not everything in nature is in decline.

The hike back to the cabin is a long one, but I have plenty of time now and force myself to slow my pace. Up here in the heights, there's enough light to walk the whole night through, and those dark clouds over Rondane don't look as if they're heading my way. Up above the willow and juniper, this is easy hiking terrain, and I wander over four of the rounded peaks, including Jammerdalshøgda, descending where I started out on February 28 this year—and in 1972. Little life is in evidence here, but the shifting light plays over Rondane as the sun comes and goes, and the rain showers move across the sky to my north.

It's actually unusual to see much life in the mountains at all, or nature of any kind. Since our expectations about the natural world are based on those spectacular TV series that condense months of effort in wildlife-rich regions, involving endless patience and cutting-edge technology, it's impossible not to be disappointed by the reality. This doesn't just apply to Norway, either: even on the savannas or in the rainforests, great, dramatic encounters with charismatic fauna are few and far between; but they're much rarer in Norwegian nature, where the high point of a forest hike may well be a squirrel sighting. Nature is scant on these barren mountain plateaus. And that isn't just because the mountains suffer from a harsh climate and poor soil quality; it is also a legacy of years of pressure from hunting, combined with increased traffic and tourism. But nature *as such* is there, and the qualities of nature that stem from everything that *isn't* there—time pressure and other demands, overcrowding, traffic jams, and light and noise pollution—are present all the same. The art lies in noticing the small within the vastness, like the moss campion's tiny, almost unnatural oases of purple on sunny, sheltered slopes against the contrasting white of star-tipped cup lichen and reindeer lichen; the burnet moth's "bloodstains" against a backdrop of black; billions of midges dancing above a willow thicket backlit by the low sun; and the buzz of bumblebees above blossoming willows.

Between two peaks, I hike across a boggy patch. I've heard the melancholy fluting of the golden plover in the distance, like a faint steam engine whistle in the night. Why do we experience it as melancholy? It has always puzzled me how soundscapes play so directly upon our states of mind. When I come closer, the golden plover resorts to its age-old trick of flying between the hillocks feigning injury and whistling urgently, thereby unintentionally announcing that its eggs or chicks lie in the opposite direction. I take out my binoculars to observe once more the elegant wader's mottled green back and dark belly, separated by the ermine white of its collar.

If I lift my gaze, I can see the shifting play of sun and clouds upon the snowy peaks in the distance. Just as it must have been fifty years ago, or five thousand. That same play of light on snow that the first wild reindeer hunters saw here, although I have no idea whether they reflected upon its *beauty*. Maybe they merely noted and assessed the weather as it pertained to hunting or the need for shelter—like a wolverine? Before romanticism laid its beautifying veil over mountains and moorland, this was often described as an inhospitable wilderness, which of course it was. Yet I still believe that the capacity to perceive nature and even mountaintops as beautiful has been with us for a long time. The fact that we find campfire sites in the particular locations where they are and probably always have been also has an aesthetic aspect; and when Bronze Age chieftains were buried in mounds on spectacular viewpoints, it was to ensure that they would be able to gaze upon these vistas for all eternity. Yet at the same time, people didn't build farms on barren, wind-blasted land because they prioritized panoramas over productivity; they didn't choose mountain hikes over reindeer hunts.

For two long days now I have hiked in the mountains, roaming from river valleys to willow thickets, to bogs, plateaus, and peaks, without seeing the wolverine—as expected. Nor have I seen any of the reindeer that I *might* have expected to come across. But the encounter with the wolf still resonates. And even without this—for me historic—meeting, I'm left contented by these two days. It's enough just to be present here; to hike soundlessly on the feathery star-tipped cup lichen, which has not yet acquired the dry brittleness that will come with summer's drought, in sight of the snowy peaks; it is enough to have all the time in the world.

Sunset is still a long way off when I arrive at my own cabin, but after ten hours on the move, I don't have much pep left. It'll be a meal-in-a-bag for me tonight (freeze-dried hiking food can be surprisingly good). So I light the stove and just sit there. Before opening a book or creeping into the bunk, I want to try spending some time in absolute inactivity. A while later, I go out onto the stoop and gaze at the pink sky in the northwest, hear that the brambling is still busy, watch the gray-brown female flycatcher sneaking into the bird box while the black-and-white male keeps watch, and I think that I really did draw a winning ticket in life. An hour easily passes in which I can't say I actually do anything. I don't much appreciate boredom per se, and think people tend to exaggerate how important it is to allow ourselves to be bored. On the other hand, I do think boredom is a motivator, in that it encourages us to find ways to avoid it. That's why children shouldn't be entertained to death but rather forced to make their own entertainment.

I count myself lucky to have grown up in a pre-digital age. In 1972, neither the internet, personal computers, nor smartphones featured on the lists of even the most imaginative futurologists. To my parents' pride, I had recently appeared in the local newspaper as "Lillehammer Library's most frequent borrower." Remedying boredom is not the primary purpose of books, although they do also fulfill that function. They give us knowledge and stimulate our imagination. As a child, I read everything; nowadays I rarely have time for anything other than scientific literature, but on the few occasions I do take the time to read for pleasure, I'm instantly flooded by images of landscapes, people, and situations. Reading brings out some of the extraordinary creativity of the dreaming brain. That's why one of the things I'm aiming to do during these days, or rather nights, in the mountains is make time to read.

Out on the stoop this particular evening, I never manage to feel bored, or at least not to feel that intense, unbearable boredom we often experience in a traffic jam or a waiting room where there are no distractions. Yet after a while, the restlessness creeps up on me. I have to do something, though not because I need to escape from the silence and my own company. On the contrary: the absence of the day-to-day noise is precisely what I've most been looking forward to. I could of course chop some wood, but I don't have the physical energy for that right now. So it's also perfectly fine to go back into the cabin after a while and sit down with John Vaillant's *The Tiger: A True Story of Vengeance and Survival.*

I'm soon transported from the local mountains, traveling with Vaillant to the easternmost outpost of Siberia—Manchuria, which borders with China, Mongolia, North Korea, and the Sea of Japan. Although tigers and wolverines have some obvious differences—not just in size, habitat, and the extent to which they pose a real danger to humans—both enjoy the status of legendary predators that few of us will be lucky enough to see in the wild. *The Tiger* takes place in the forested taiga, which combines astonishing lushness with the notoriously harsh Siberian winters. This is a hunt that goes both ways: humans hunt the tiger, but the opposite is also true. The tiger's legendary status stems from its literal embodiment of massive primal power, combined with a talent for invisibility. "The general appearance of the tiger is that of a huge physical force and quiet confidence, combined with a rather heavy grace," writes Vaillant—citing the encyclopedia reference from

Mammals of the Soviet Union. He then expands on this, spicing up the description:

> To properly appreciate such an animal, it is most instructive to start at the beginning: picture the grotesquely muscled head of a pit bull and then imagine how it might look if the pit bull weighed a quarter of a ton. Add to this fangs the length of a finger backed up by rows of slicing teeth capable of cutting through the heaviest bone. Consider then the claws: a hybrid of meat hook and stiletto that can attain four inches along the outer curve, a length comparable to the talons on a velociraptor. Now imagine the vehicle for all this: nine feet or more from nose to tail, and three and a half feet high at the shoulder. Finally, emblazon this beast with a primordial calligraphy: black brushstrokes on a field of russet and cream, and wonder at our strange fortune to coexist with such a creature.[22]

Even the wolverine falls short of this, of course. Yet its essence is the same: the perfect adaptation of the predator, manifested in some species more than others through a compact display of power and invisibility. This sets the predator apart from the large herbivores, which, to put it somewhat disrespectfully, are nothing but eating machines constructed around the vast digestive system required to wring nutrition out of their meager plant-based diet. But because predators are competitors that operate in the same niche as us, and are also—biologically speaking—a step above us on the food chain, they have historically been objects of hatred. The Siberian tiger, the subspecies Vaillant is writing about, is the world's largest feline, but this creature that once ruled over vast swaths of eastern Russia, northeast China, and North Korea has now been reduced to probably fewer than a thousand individuals, the majority of them in captivity. Despite its own woes, the wolverine is better off in several respects: not only does it occupy large stretches of the boreal zone, both forest and mountain regions, but humans are not on its menu, and it doesn't have the misfortune to feature in traditional Chinese medicine. Tigers and wolverines both symbolize what we have lost in nature: our fear and respect for it, our fascination and wonder, but first and foremost, the wildness. Both are now tamed, their claws and canines drawn, but they still exist out there and may very occasionally be encountered, like mythical creatures of old that serve to remind us of what we are in the process of losing.

The summer heat has not yet come and the cold seeps into the cabin. I fetch Dad's old woolen sweater from the closet. It has holes in the elbows, just like all the best cabin sweaters. Then I wander over to the outhouse and chop some kindling from a couple of logs. The axe is as sharp as a scythe blade—Dad knew how to whet axes too. I light the stove, feed three large logs into it, and adjust the draw to a minimum so it'll burn for as long as possible, offering a modicum of heat in the early hours. I lie for a while listening to the steady roar of the stove, then I briefly listen out for mice in the walls. I hear none, and besides I've barely seen any rodents. That doesn't bode well for the rough-legged buzzards' breeding season.

Toward dawn, I have a strange dream, one I used to have often as a boy but which I had forgotten entirely. The dream was rooted in reality: one time on a forest hike with Dad we'd found a spot where several used cars had been dumped. People had come along and broken them up in search of usable parts, and I saw a beautiful long, shiny, copper object lying on the ground. A dynamo, Dad explained, adding some detail about how it worked. Dad knew everything, after all. I lifted it up, utterly perplexed by the weight, which bore no reasonable relationship to its size. Later, this shining, spinning dynamo regularly returned to me in peculiar dreams, actually just as much emotions as dreams, in which my body became strangely heavy and rotated at a dizzying speed. I now recall the last time I had this dream, too: it was after Dad and I found the wolverine track in 1972 and I learned about the animal's almost magical qualities—as I understood it back then. Then, as now, I recalled that indescribable sensation of spinning weight, which became associated in some peculiar way with the wolverine and the disproportionate relationship between its size and strength. I lie there for a long time, trying to hold on to the dream and the feeling, but the light that filters in through the thin curtains gradually erases them. The spring orchestra outside struck up long before.

ON THIS PARTICULAR DAY, too, I'm going on a kind of sentimental journey. It was almost cold enough for frost last night, and it's still chilly when I hike south from the cabin along a ridge that descends fairly steeply toward the bog in the east. I haven't gone more than a few hundred yards when a flapping black grouse hen suddenly careens through the undergrowth in front of me. She stops briefly to assess the situation before flapping helplessly onward along the ground. This diversion might have worked if it weren't for the five or six heedless balls of fluff that came dashing along in her wake, yellowish brown and cheeping. Lucky for them I'm not a fox. Just afterward, another game bird flies up, the only ptarmigan I've seen these past few days, although there's no sign that it has a nest here.

I follow the slope for a while before turning off, this time westward, along a lengthy stretch of bog, promisingly white with cloudberry flowers, then on through dense birch scrub and across another bog until a rock face looms up behind the forest. From here, I continue carefully through the woodland, expecting at any moment to hear the unmistakable screech of the rough-legged buzzard before it swoops over my head on its broad wings. When that happens I'll beat a retreat, confident that it seems to have found its way back to its old nesting place. But the screech never comes, and I walk all the way up to the rock face. Neither of the two nesting ledges are occupied, and they appear not to have been for several years. Small bushes and plants are growing nicely in what remains of the old nests, well fertilized by the remnants of the buzzards' prey and their excrement. This was hardly unexpected: rough-legged buzzards don't bother to breed unless they have access to plentiful food. There has been little of that for many years, as small-rodent populations have been peaking more infrequently, and there isn't much ptarmigan to supplement the buzzards' diet. However, I have a task to perform here.

The summer after my first encounter with the wolverine tracks by the peaks of Jammerdal, I managed, with

Dad's help, to hang up a sawn-off, hollow log in a thick-trunked old spruce at the end of a small tarn beyond the buzzard's cliff. This was the conclusion of a lengthy and labor-intensive project. The previous fall, I had come across a fallen spruce, old, dried out, and hollow on the inside—or partly so—but still hard on the outside. I widened the space with a chisel, then bored and sawed a cavity that would be the perfect size for any boreal owl that could find enough mice here to make it worth breeding, or else a common goldeneye if an owl hadn't already claimed the spot. Then I nailed a base onto it and fitted it with a removable roof. It was a solid and very heavy object when finished, and it cost us considerable sweat and a few drops of blood to get the monster all the way here and then up the tree. Once up, though, it would hang there for the benefit of ducks and owls for years to come. Ducks did nest there for a few years, but after a while I never seemed to have time to come here during breeding season, and now it's been several decades since my last visit. It's unlikely to be hanging here still after fifty years, but maybe I can find some archaeological remains at the foot of the tree.

There are a few ancient, thick-trunked spruces scattered around here, probably a couple of centuries old or more. I'm pretty certain which one of these it was, an old giant with a forked trunk, but I find no sign of a bird box either in or under the tree. I peer up along the trunk beneath the skirts of the spruce. Nothing there either, and suddenly fifty years feels like a terribly long time ago. Can every trace really have been erased? Surely there must be *something* left? Beyond this tree, another giant has fallen—could it have been that one? Here, wood fungi have set up shop in the fallen trunk, especially red-belted conk, but there's no sign of the bird box anywhere. It makes me oddly sad. Not that it *means* anything whether or not this bird box still exists, and of course I don't expect it still to be hanging there—but can all traces of our efforts, mine and Dad's, have been so thoroughly eradicated, as if they had happened in another world? Well, perhaps they did.

And then I find it after all. It's hanging in a tree closer to the lake than I'd recalled, and looks exactly the same as fifty years ago! I climb up and see that the years have made their mark. Externally it looks surprisingly unchanged, but under the lid, decay has taken its toll, thanks to insects and rot. The opposite applies to me, I think. Externally, I can see that the years have passed, but on a good day, I can feel that I'm still the same inside. The box may not still be hanging here another ten years from now, yet it gives me an irrational rush of happiness to be connected to my past like this. I remember a photo Dad took of me up the tree beside the bird box once we'd managed to maneuver it into place. As I ponder where this picture might be, I pull out my cell phone and take a selfie with the bird box.

Afterward, I hike on over a pretty little mountain that stands here like an outpost, barely raising its white lichen-clad head above the tree line, and offering a view of the rather serious mountains to the east and the truly serious mountains of Rondane, as well as a glimpse of the legendary Jotunheimen. This particular mountain, Skarfjell—whose name refers to a nearby cleft in the terrain—has always served as a regular winter habitat for ptarmigans, but I cross the highest parts of it a few times without seeing any sign of these birds before descending the steep mountainside in an easterly direction. Hiking down a slope like this, with passages between cliffs as well as dead ends that lead to steep precipices, is a bit like finding a decent skiing route on dwindling snow in springtime. There's a particular pleasure to be had from reading the terrain correctly. I have no problem finding a path down to Svarttjern. There are three reasons that a body of water might have this name, which means "black tarn": either it's a dark bog lake, or there aren't any fish (*black* in such cases may imply *devoid of*), or there actually *are* fish. In the latter case, the point of the name would be to convince other anglers that there's nothing to catch here, thereby avoiding competition.

Back when we set up the large bird box, Dad and I also released some trout into this lake. It's not the kind of thing you're supposed to do, because it can cause pollution by non-native species and populations, but in those days, it was seen as a commendable activity that was part of a tradition dating back thousands of years. There's barely a single mountain lake where people *haven't* introduced fish, and angling clubs around the country continue this practice, known as cultivation. Nature was for harvesting, and anything that aided this was an indisputable benefit. Planting forests, digging ditches, and draining bogs were all necessary actions if we were to put nature to work for our ends. Wasn't that the whole point of nature, after all? To be cultivated and harvested. If not, it would simply lie around uselessly, so cultivation was a vocation and a duty, and, to some extent, a necessity of life. This recurs as a central idea all the way from Christian doctrines of dominance and stewardship to natural teleology to modern-day nature management. According to this view, there were useful and non-useful animals, as well as pests or beasts—like the wolverine. In the mid-nineteenth century, the Norwegian government passed a law aimed at eliminating predators and protecting other wildlife, which established that all predatory animals—including birds of prey—should simply be wiped out. Thanks to bounty payments and high fur prices, the bear and wolf were almost eradicated from Norway's fauna, and the bell was also tolling for lynxes and wolverines by the time protective measures were introduced fifty years ago. The wolverine was protected in southern Norway in 1973, even though in reality it had already been wiped out in that part of the country by then. In other words, the wolverine track Dad and I came across in 1972 really *was* a rarity. No new litters were born in southern Norway until the end of the 1970s. In 1982, the wolverine was also protected in the rest of the country—to a degree. As I mentioned earlier, a ceiling of thirty-nine wolverine litters per year has been established. License hunting was introduced in the north of Norway in 1993 and the south of Norway in 1997. Over the past ten years on record, between 61 and 157 wolverines have been shot annually (the statistics refer to this as "mortality"). The difficulty of getting within shooting range of a wolverine accounts for the practice of taking out female wolverines and cubs at the den. At the time of writing, the wolverine population was estimated to stand at 386 individuals. This is actually pretty close to the estimated 400 individuals in the contiguous United States! Rare in Norway, even rarer in America.

Eradication is one issue, introduction quite another. Releasing fish into lakes that previously had none was once an uncontroversial cultivation strategy aimed at getting more out of nature; in the early years, the fish populations can achieve spectacular growth as they feast off a fauna that—from the harvesting perspective—consists of uninteresting and far-from-charismatic creatures like insects, crustaceans, and mollusks. The disappearance of the beautiful fairy shrimps (which swim gracefully through the water upside down as the light glances off their paddling legs in all the colors of the rainbow), along with other species—such as the utterly fascinating horseshoe-crab-like Arctic tadpole shrimps, dragonflies, predacious diving beetles, and daphnia—seemed like a purely academic issue. And for the most part, that probably still holds true to this day, although the realization that species we don't eat also have value has gained a foothold in nature management practice and legislation.

The notion that fairy shrimps and Arctic tadpole shrimps are significant per se, and that nature could have an intrinsic value that restricts our own rights over it, is an exceptionally radical one in the context of our traditional approach to nature, which is based on concepts of management, rights holders, and harvesting. Rooted in pantheism, the intrinsic value of nature is not an entirely alien concept from a historical perspective, although it was previously based on the notion that nature is endowed with a spirit or forms part of a creation. But how can the fairy shrimp, produced solely through the workings of evolution, possess a value that is not assigned by us? On the other hand, both it and its distant relative, the Arctic tadpole shrimp, have been here for 300 million years—or at least we have fossils dating back that far that are suspiciously similar to their current forms. From this standpoint, they can at least be said to have a certain time-honored entitlement to existence, especially compared with us humans, who have only been around for 300,000 years. The two species also came here to the Norwegian mountains long before us, and long before we began to fill the lakes with fish, or at least those lakes that fish had not managed to reach alone. Just the dizzying horizons of time encompassed within these and other life-forms ought to be enough to earn them a right of residence in the mountains. The Arctic tadpole shrimp and the fairy shrimp still have a few scattered refuges in mountain lakes or pools that are too shallow or narrow to support other life. Yet they are far from secure, because a lot has happened to the climate in the past fifty years too. In Dovre, northwest of the Rondane Mountains, where there are more fairy shrimp, the species has disappeared from all locations between the altitudes of roughly 3,000 and 3,600 feet over this period, although they are still clinging on at higher altitudes. Notably, the average temperature at the altitudes where fairy shrimp have vanished has crept up over the same time period.

Nature *does* have an intrinsic value; only someone with a boundlessly anthropocentric attitude could claim otherwise. It's just something other than the utility value we assign to it. Admittedly no one except us could say that a mountain was beautiful or a view splendid, but our gaze is just one among thousands. Nature as a whole is seething with vitality quite independent of us and our gaze. Of course the wolverine has value.

Dad and I spoke about most things, and a great deal about nature. He came from a harvesting culture in which fishing, seabird hunting, and egg foraging were not leisure pursuits but a crucial means of sourcing food. Even so, he was an early advocate of conservation, although we never discussed whether releasing fish into a genuinely fish-free lake might be a crime against the humble fauna beneath the surface that neither of us were aware of at the time. If we'd thought that thought, I'm pretty certain we would have dropped our private cultivation program. We had passed by here several times and never seen any sign of circles on the water or anglers, so we concluded that the lake was "dead" and therefore an ideal spot to release fry that we could harvest in the years to come. For one reason or another, we never did return to see the results of our attempt, and I'm not expecting there to be any fish here now, given the lack of a proper spawning stream. That disadvantage was the reason why we unsuccessfully tried to get hold of some Arctic char back then, as they spawn in lakes and don't need a spawning stream, unlike trout.

I'm jerked back to the present when a circle suddenly appears in the water right in front of me. It's not a huge trout but apparently sizable enough to be worth frying. It isn't necessarily a descendant of the fish we released; others may have been introduced into the lake both before and after our attempt, and I now see that there actually *is* an outlet stream that could support a modest population of spawning fish.

A male common scoter flaps up from an islet in the lake, right beside the outlet stream. The knoll is just big enough for a duck's nest and encircled by reeds. This doesn't come as any great surprise, since I'd already spotted the coal-black male out on the lake from some way off. The polar opposite of the northern phalarope male, he happily leaves all the drudgery and responsibility of raising the young to the female. I once saw an Arctic loon out on this lake too, after hearing its characteristic wail from up on the mountainside. It was probably roosting on the same islet the common scoter has laid claim to this year, since that seems to be the only possible nesting place on the lake. That sighting was duly written down along with my other nature notes—with an exclamation mark. The Arctic loon doesn't just have an unusual cry, it is also an uncommonly beautiful bird: it has a gray head with zebra stripes along the neck and beneath the beak; a dark burgundy neckerchief above a white breast that gives way to more zebra stripes along the side; and its dark back is covered in intricate white patterns like stripes and patches. The extravagance of the songs, plumage, and courtship dances of many bird species shows just what a powerful engine of evolution sexual selection can be.

Today, I've decided to leave the wolverine to its own devices and stick to the forest, where I follow a route I've never taken before. In the southwest, jutting out from the southern flank of Skarfjell, I've seen a series of rocky terraces that lead down to a few splendid fishing lakes, one of which is home to some fine Arctic char. I don't have my rod with me today, so the appeal right now is the pleasure of hiking in new terrain—and curiosity about these small cliffs. They form what looks like a gigantic staircase down from the peak behind me, its steps somewhat irregularly placed. First of all, I hike back up from the lake again, though farther south than the point I previously descended from. The biggest cliff is here, and as I approach, I encounter a rough-legged buzzard. It screeches twice and wheels high above my head but then vanishes quietly into the bare mountains to the east. There's no sign of nests, and after a while I see that this rock face isn't suitable for rough-legged buzzards. It's too low and too gentle, without any sheer sections or overhangs, so a fox could easily make its way up to any nest that was built here. But the buzzard is in the vicinity; that's something.

I hike up along the rock face, and once I'm nearly at the top, I follow a broad "step" on the birch-clad hillside around to the southern side. Here, I zigzag back down through a dense forest of birch interspersed with the occasional pine, descending to the next broad ledge. I've never enjoyed traipsing around down in the forest as much as hiking in the mountains. You're closed in here and there's no view; you don't get the same sense of freedom. The forest is fine as second best—but of course not all forests are equal. For example, young, dense, even-aged spruce forest offers a sad, dark, and species-poor experience compared with a rugged, old, mixed forest that is more open and lets the light in. But my favorite woodland is highest up: sparse downy birch forests with the occasional rough, ancient pine. That kind of forest will give you a sense of freedom. And the mountain is always right behind it.

This particular stretch of woodland is almost mountain forest, but it's sheltered from wind and weather on a sun-warmed mountainside, and these benign conditions have resulted in overly dense growth. Spruce has really taken hold here and is supplanting the birch, shutting out both light and view. Yet I sense that it's opening up there ahead of me where the next cliff must be. I walk carefully out onto the edge and lie down on my stomach with my binoculars. It isn't a massive drop—it would hardly satisfy the raven's demands for an inaccessible roost, or the rough-legged buzzard's or the falcon's for that matter. And there are no nests to be seen either, nor are there any white stripes of guano down below. Still, it's a nice place to lie quietly for a while. I look into the legendary bare mountains, wishing I'd taken a hike there instead. Somewhat closer to hand I catch a glimpse of the Breia, which has now reached the end of its wild intermezzo of falls and rapids and found its way back to the calmer course that will take it due south until it encounters steeper terrain once more. Directly below lies the lake containing Arctic char, although I can only see its far shore. I lie like this and scout the terrain until a bug crawls across my arm. I let it roam for a while before carefully tipping it into the heather. A minute later, it's back on my arm. This time I flick it a bit harder and it vanishes over the edge. Three minutes later, it's on my arm again. I'm clearly irresistible.

Since it's too early for mosquitoes, my own patience is the only factor limiting how long I can lie here watching, or mostly listening out for signs of life. Patience has never been my strong suit and it's diminished with age. I've gotten used to always being in a hurry, so I need to train this skill up again. It's the middle of the day and a quiet time. After a while, I hear something trampling around down there in the dense forest, probably a moose, since I've seen plenty of moose dung on this hillside, some of it very fresh. I can hear it increasingly clearly but can't see anything. That's the curse of the forest: it hides everything. After fifteen minutes, I continue along the edge of the cliff and find a pleasant descent to the next ledge. From here, I skirt Skarfjell, returning to the place where I first ascended, and I'm back at the cabin by the early afternoon. I give the place a cursory sweep and tidy because I'll be the one to come here next, and besides there's not much point doing too much cleaning at the cabin. A cabin is meant to be used, and a spot of dust on the floor won't do anyone any harm.

After I return from the mountains this time, I get a message from Eivind, who took me wolverine spotting in the winter. Since the snow has melted, they've visited the area we went to so they could confirm or rule out the presence of a litter. Eight yards or so below the hole in the snow, in a tunnel system some forty yards long, everything indicates that wolverine cubs were indeed there this year: fur, tooth marks on twigs, wolverine latrines, and wear and tear on the vegetation. The likelihood that wolverine cubs lay here on that slope beneath the snow is a real boost. I was *so* close. *And I saw a wolf.*

Summer

At midsummer, we have to do as the reindeer does: seek out the snow and the highest ground. Here it's still cool, even on warm days, and you can escape the worst and most persistent stinging insects. And yes, although I'm concerned about the decline in insect numbers and see these species as a necessary benefit for the agricultural ecosystem, I'm no fan of mosquitoes, flies, or horseflies. But I still take a short trip to the cabin in mid-August. In June, the cloudberry blossom was promisingly abundant, and that gives me a great excuse to come back. During the last month of summer, you get the sense that nature is breathing a sigh of relief after a hectic youth. The chicks have left the nest and are largely self-sufficient. At the same time, the days are warm and all living things can roam around relatively free of care, harvesting the fruits of summer. The cold fall is still a long way off, and September is also an excellent month for seed and berry eaters. For thrushes, this is the high season, when they fly into the mountains in restless flocks and eat ripe berries.

The insect eaters have long been uneasy: the fall colors in every shade of red and yellow that are beautiful to us serve as warning signs to them. The fall leaves speak of night frosts and empty platters, even though insects still buzz around on southern slopes on sunny days, and the midges may still dance over bushes and trees. As the insect-eating birds leave, silence gradually descends over the mountains, and when the last flocks of thrushes fly to lower-lying regions in early October, the mountains are strangely dead and quiet.

Even by early August, a kind of melancholy calm already lies over the mountains, although they may be brimming with berries and still full of life. It's quiet because there's no longer any reason to sing, and I catch myself missing the busyness and noise of spring and early summer. The bright green, fresh chlorophyll of those earlier days has taken on a grayish tinge, especially noticeable after wet summers, when the greenery is colonized by microscopic fungi. Most people think of cap mushrooms when the talk turns to fungi, but those visible manifestations of an extensive subterranean network represent just a tiny fraction of the fungi in nature.

It is impossible not to link the annual cycle of nature to the course of my own life. I am in the August of my years at best, yet it still gives me an intense joy to hike over the bogland and feel my body working. And this is what I'm doing now. I've long known the destination of today's hike. As so often before, I head southward from the cabin and take the quickest route across the short stretches of bog, grabbing some cloudberries along the way without taking the time to stop and pick more. The annual cloudberry lottery in August is always an event I greet with childish delight, and cloudberries are the only berries I think it's fun to pick. But berry picking is only the pretext for my hike this time, even though I brought along enough buckets in my bag to carry home twenty pounds if the opportunity arises. For now, though, I'll eat my fill on my way to the big bog, Stormyra. I found a fantastic haul of berries there one fall.

People either love or hate cloudberries; some think they taste of watery bog and are full of pips, but others—like me—relish the incredible taste of sweetness, of sun, mountains, and yes, maybe bogland too, but in a positive sense. It's like ptarmigan breast, which also, in some inexplicable way, tastes of mountains and wildness; for me, cloudberries are to garden berries what ptarmigan breast is to a bloodless, flavorless chicken breast. Or champagne to bock beer, as the philosopher and naturalist Peter Wessel Zapffe said when comparing mountain climbing to other sports. I turn down into the cleft beside Skarfjell and once again cross the river valley via a stretch of bog. I spy some cloudberries out of the corner of my eye but resist the distraction. On the track to Breistølen summer farm, I pass an old man outside an even older cottage. Axe in hand, he walks purposefully toward a chopping block with split logs on one side and unsplit logs on the other. The wind plays in his snow-white downy hair. He has the characteristically stiff gait of the old—dodgy knees and a slightly bent back—and his mouth hangs half open, as if he's intent on the task at hand. Chopping wood: the old man's last contribution to useful citizenship. He doesn't notice me, just places a fresh log on the block, lifts the axe above his head, and splits it the first time. It didn't look like an especially powerful blow, but this is a man who has split many a log and sharpened many an axe in his time. Then he takes a little breather before setting up the next log. I unconsciously straighten my own back and walk on with artificially long, efficient, energetic strides.

When, a while later, I solemnly pass the spot where I saw the almost-certainly-a-wolf cross my path in June, I find four goat kids standing there, which stop grazing briefly to stare at me with big eyes. Then I cross the Breia and walk two-thirds of a mile through boggy birch forest until I'm out on Stormyra. It's a pretty long march, this, but I'm gradually finding my way back to the joy of being on the move, the joy of walking. I still need a goal but, as we all know, the journey itself is often the best part: the curse lies in reaching your destination.

Parts of the bog area here are wetlands covered in yellow bottle sedge. The bog is no fun, but there are some drier sections here and there, especially on the outer edges toward the birch forest, where there are peat and cloudberry bogs. The trouble with cloudberries is that the weather can't be too dry or too wet, too warm or too cold, and a single night of frost can destroy the whole lot. Consequently, you can find pockets in the terrain, on the edges of forests, or along the dampest stretches where the berries abound, whereas open areas are empty. This year, there was a frosty night when the cloudberries were blossoming, so those mountain bogs that burgeoned with promising flowers in early summer are now bare. The cloudberry leaves remain, resigned, part brown, part red, without a single berry to show. It is a peculiarity of the species that it has this masochistic tendency to grow over large swaths of the northern hemisphere but only produces berries here in the cold north, where it has every chance of failing.

I start to walk across the bog. Walking has long been a much-praised activity—some even claim it's the essence of life. Although walking is something I do primarily to get from A to B, as the years have passed, I have begun to feel that it does have an intrinsic value, that it is an *autotelic* experience. And walking across a boggy landscape with a spring in my step, downy birch around me, and the mountains to my rear certainly gives me a particular kind of peace.

"I wish to speak a word for Nature," writes Thoreau in his essay "Walking," "for absolute freedom and wildness, as contrasted with a freedom and culture merely civil..."[23] before embarking on a homage to walking rather than nature itself. For Thoreau, walking is the goal.

> I think that I cannot preserve my health and spirits, unless I spend four hours a day at least—and it is commonly more than that—sauntering through the woods and over the hills and fields, absolutely free from all worldly engagements. You may safely say, A penny for your thoughts, or a thousand pounds. When sometimes I am reminded that the mechanics and shopkeepers stay in their shops not only all the forenoon, but all the afternoon too, sitting with crossed legs, so many of them—as if the legs were made to

> sit upon, and not to stand or walk upon—I think that they deserve some credit for not having all committed suicide long ago.[24]

If I had been one of those shopkeepers, I'd have been pretty irritated by Thoreau's romantic arrogance—after all, who can live off birdsong, fresh air, and walking? No one who has a family to care for, at any rate. And even without practical or duty-ethical reasons to keep going in a more prosaic sense, it's difficult to regard walking as life's most meaningful project. Existence must contain something beyond pastimes, it must be about *achieving* something too, about making some contribution to our fellow humans and the future.

But Thoreau's point is perhaps not that we should always be walking, but rather that we should all take the time to experience things. If the shopkeeper exchanged 20 percent of his income for the opportunity to take a meditative hike in nature, he would acquire a richer life. Some of the most active and *high-achieving* people appreciate walking in part because walking and slow time can be seen as an investment in mental energy. It pays off. Walking can be *heterotelic*, in other words, a *means* to achieving a goal, or getting to a given place. But it also has a value per se because it shares some of the qualities of a good night's sleep. It isn't "wasted" time. Erling Kagge, polar explorer, publisher, and author, cites Milan Kundera's observation: "The degree of slowness is directionally proportional to the intensity of memory; the degree of speed is directionally proportional to the intensity of forgetting." When we try to remember something as we walk, we automatically slow down. Perhaps we also think more richly and deeply at a slower pace. Personally, I've never really analyzed my feelings about walking, other than that I like to do it on the way to something. In my daily life, I always walk quickly, faster as I grow older, I feel. Few things better reflect the increased speed of life than the pace at which we walk. Perhaps it's also to do with the fact that we're busier, as well as the sense that we have less and less time left. There is so much to be done and "each day brings more tasks than the last." Closer to home, I go running out in nature, and my speed doesn't necessarily detract from the thoughts and ideas I have along the way. Besides, the advantage of moving fast is that you can cover more terrain. I couldn't have hiked around extensive bog and mountain areas if I hadn't been going at quite a lick, and walking with long, tireless strides across bogs, hills, and mountains is a joy in its own right. The rambler's gait. But there's a major difference between walking on asphalt on your way to something and roaming across bogs and plateaus. *Strolling* is an urban exercise, generally involving short steps on sidewalks. For me, walking is something entirely different. In my youth, I walked far and often in the mountains, and even though I was always on my way to or from something, the walking was always about more than simple transportation. As I walk across the bogs here, I rediscover this joy of walking. I'm on my way to the bare mountain, but I'm simultaneously taking pleasure in walking here; I am both present and en route.

Stormyra, the big bog, belongs to a large, partly connected complex of bogs. To avoid disturbing the cranes, I walk along the forest that borders its northern edge. I've seen the little family through my binoculars: mother, father, and their long-legged offspring. The cloudberries are a disappointment this year, though. Either they blossomed later, after the frosty night, or the temperature rose just above the critical point. The few berries I do find are large, yellowish red, and delicate. After picking one here and another there, I find I've actually managed to collect a pound or so. I've never seen any animals or birds eating cloudberries, although the sweet, juicy, enticingly colored packaging is an unmistakable strategy to ensure ingestion and dispersal of the hard seeds. Blueberries are the bear's main source of nutrition from late summer until hibernation—massive amounts of blueberries. Scientists who have studied this kind of thing claim that bears will also grab some cloudberries when they get a chance. But what about the wolverine? Since it eats everything, it probably wouldn't turn down any cloudberries it happened across. It's a mystery to me why most birds here don't gorge on them, but blueberries are the thing as far as they're concerned. They even seem to prefer the flavorless crowberry, although cloudberries do appear to be on the menu for both thrushes and ptarmigans.

Part of the joy of bogland for me is precisely the fact that it serves up my favorite berries in the fall, but it has so many other qualities too. Bogs are underrated ecosystems that have traditionally been seen as utterly useless until they have been drained, cultivated, and ultimately planted with forest. Bogs are carbon stores, water stores, and unique ecosystems, and they also smell fresh and good in their own particular way. Many people think of bogs as unclean, or even downright rotten. In fact the opposite is true—as the wolverine knows: it uses the bog both as refrigerator and antiseptic larder. A reindeer thigh buried in a bog will keep splendidly for weeks. Bog bodies that have been found in places where people cut peat may look as if they ended up in the bog just weeks earlier, whereas they've actually spent a thousand years down there amid the oxygen-deprived remains of the moss. While the birch-covered hills and mountainsides to the left of my field of vision have accumulated barely any soil since the Ice Age, many feet of black, carbon-rich bog soil lie beneath me.

Thoreau also wrote a lot about bogs:

> Hope and the future for me are not in lawns and cultivated fields, not in towns and cities, but in the impervious and quaking swamps ... Yes, though you may think me perverse, if it were proposed to me to dwell in the neighborhood of the most beautiful garden that ever human art contrived, or else of a Dismal swamp, I should certainly decide for the swamp.[25]

Well, that doesn't give us any insight into what makes bogs attractive, and it's hard to see how they offer hope and future. For me, their appeal is that the open landscape instills a sense of calm; and, as with so much else in nature, what is absent can be just as important as what is present. Yet bogs can also be genuinely beautiful when the cotton grass spreads out before you like a white carpet backlit by the sun, or when grayleaf willow and silvery-green sedge encircle tiny mirrorlike pools, or when the different species of peat moss form a patchwork in a variety of hues: bright green haircap moss, but, above all, peat mosses in shades that range from green to the deep crimson of the northern and red varieties. And once you start looking closer, you'll find buckbean, purple cinquefoil, mounds of deer grass, bog bilberry, grayleaf willow, and other members of the *Salix* genus whose names I can barely remember, as well as club sedge, bottle sedge, and their many relatives; dwarf birch, of course; marsh lousewort, the heather that is now in full bloom; patches of star-tipped cup lichen in the driest areas; and Arctic kidney lichen, a peculiar species that looks like large leaves—to name but a few. The edges of the bog are lined with wolfsbane, its upper third in bloom. This smart species flowers successively over several weeks so it will have a greater chance of benefiting from any periods of good weather.

A large expanse of the bog stretches farther south, but I'm keen to head higher. After one and a half hours hiking mostly in bogland interspersed only occasionally with stands of birch, I gradually climb into higher and increasingly drier terrain. The forest becomes sparser. To the south lies Veslefjell, "Little Mountain," which is a fine and striking peak despite its unassuming name. On the other side lies Øverlihøgda. I halt for a while, weighing up the pros and cons. The advantage of Øverlihøgda is that it takes me farther into the mountains along a high ridge that follows the Breia River on its southern side, in toward the reindeer grave and the wolverine talus, which will offer a hope of seeing reindeer, at least. I leave my bag hanging on the birch that's highest up, which should make it easy to find again, and take along only binoculars, packed lunch, and a thin windbreaker. Once again I hike over these hills, passing the plane wreck and trying unsuccessfully to find the reindeer grave again. I know it was on one of these small ridges that run north to south, but it's like looking for a needle in a haystack. As I walk, a rough-legged buzzard alights from a mound and wheels overhead before flying onward into the mountains. This is unmistakably a raptor mound, a place that birds of prey may have been using for millennia to pick clean and eat their prey, and as an excellent lookout post. I find a few pellets and some feathers, but nothing to indicate a recent catch. There are no small rodents in the mountains, and I haven't yet seen a single ptarmigan. The ground is dry as tinder here on the plateaus, but I still manage to scare up a northern harrier, a male with characteristic blue-gray wings. I go over to the place where it took off, but there's no sign of a catch here either. Pickings have probably been slim for raptors and predators in the mountains this summer.

Up in the heights, I seek shelter from the increasing wind in a south-facing spot with a place to rest my back and a view across the open highland bogs toward Storkvien. South of that peak a mysterious valley of old-growth forest descends toward Imsdalen. Dad and I once started to explore it but soon realized it was a two-day project at least. I'll make time for it at some point.

I can't spot the remains of the big buck up by Gråhøgda, but as soon as I turn my binoculars toward the lower flank of Storkvien, I see the reindeer herd. There must be close to a hundred of them, including many seriously large bucks, but there are also plenty of calves from the latest breeding season. In all, the interconnected herd to which these deer belong numbers 2,300 animals, and they sometimes migrate as far south as this mountain range extends, roughly seventy miles away. But this is their heartland and one of the places where this wildest of wild reindeer herds runs the least risk of encountering holiday cabins, highways, and humans. The reindeer seem to perceive these as genuine boundaries in the landscape, created by their main predator. Thus far, but no farther.

A raven flaps overhead pursued by two kestrels, like a heavy bomber and two nimble fighter jets. The raven appears utterly unbothered by the situation, and the kestrels mostly seem to be playing. When a couple more falcons turn up, the original two lose interest in the raven and all four play together, swooping acrobatically along a cliff in the headwinds. I interpret the activity as sheer play, but could this be a nuclear family whose youngsters are being trained by the adults? If so, the younger birds were probably the ones pestering the raven, mischievous like all youngsters. I spend the next few minutes alternating my attention between kestrels and reindeer. I sit there quietly, so far away from the herd that they can't sense my presence. Hunting season isn't far off, but this is the best time of year for reindeer. There have already been a few chilly nights, so deerflies, horseflies, and botflies are on the wane. The heat is no longer oppressive, but there's plenty of grazing, even though the plants aren't as nutrient-rich and tasty as in spring. Reindeer must enjoy life while they can. Soon they'll face the stress and anxiety of the hunting season, and after that, an endless, harsh winter with poor grazing beneath the snow. As long as there *is* snow, they cope perfectly well, but in recent winters, mild weather interspersed with frost has caused ice to form over their grazing areas. That's bad news for everything from small rodents to reindeer. There was remarkably little snow last winter, not even enough to cover the juniper bushes, whose tops are still brown from drought and frost damage.

This spot where I sit scouting for reindeer has almost certainly been used by hunters before me over millennia. Even though I'm not hunting now, I can easily imagine the excitement a reindeer hunter must have felt a thousand years ago as he and the rest of his group drove the reindeer in toward the leading fences and onward to the stone grave. Or the anticipation of those who lay hidden to the rear with bows, arrows, and spears. It was a matter of life or death for both hunter and hunted, whether the hunters were humans or wolverines.

There's a movement in the herd I'm watching through my binoculars. Those lying lower on the hillside stand up and peer downhill. Their unrest spreads, and eventually the entire herd drifts slowly and steadily along the flank of Storkvien before heading to the summit, where many of them stand for a while, silhouetted against the sky. I can't see any people over there, but something has unsettled the animals. It *may* have been a wolverine, but it'll take more than luck to spot that dark hunter in such hilly terrain from my current position. And besides, it isn't all that common for them to kill reindeer, at least not healthy specimens. The wolverine isn't a picky eater; no animal that has to survive here in the mountains can afford to be. It eats everything, but most of all carrion. It's part of nature's cleanup crew, as we often say—in line with teleological tradition—when we want to explain how everything in nature makes itself useful. What's the point of mosquitoes, for example, especially the stinging variety? They're important food for small birds, we'll say, as if that should be a reason for their existence. Besides, that answer's only partly true, considering that midges are much more important in this respect and don't suck anyone's blood. How about mice and rats? Important food for many, of course, but that isn't why they exist, any more than the wolverine has been appointed by a wise creator to keep the mountains free of stinking carrion. It does so all the same, and is capable of repurposing rotten reindeer flesh into compact wolverine muscles—although it's actually more impressive by far that the reindeer can convert nutrient-poor lichen into reindeer flesh.

Besides, the wolverine can, in theory, eat any herbivore, and it also kills sheep, sometimes a great many of them. From the wolverine's point of view, a sheep is almost as easy to get its claws on as carrion, the lowest-hanging four-legged fruit in the mountains. Sixty-five percent of all Norwegian sheep slain by predators are killed by wolverines and lynxes. Wolverines, lynxes, and golden eagles are also responsible for almost all reindeer killings by predators; in some parts of Gudbrandsdalen and Northern Norway, the wolverine is seen as the embodiment of the devil himself. Yet we are the ones who filled the mountains with sheep and then demanded that the predators whose natural habitat this is should leave them in peace.

Wolverine populations are always sparse. In North America the animal is a source of great fascination, partly because there, as here, it is seen as a dark, primal force that is known to exist but never seen, and partly because of the general rule that value increases as numbers dwindle. The wolverine is so extremely rare in most parts of North America as to support biologist E. O. Wilson's claim that you're as likely to see a unicorn as a wolverine in the wild. Yet the wolverine does exist, we know that. At roughly the same time as I was battling through the gales here in early March, Rebecca Watters, director of the Wolverine Foundation, posted an enthusiastic update on *The Wolverine Blog* under the heading "Return of the Wolverines": "It's been a pretty big week for wolverine sightings in the U.S. Rockies. A wolverine was spotted in Yellowstone National Park last week, and another in Lewistown, Montana, a few days ago."[26] But in Montana too the wolverine is a rare visitor; indeed, even Yellowstone, whose 3,500 square miles of mountains and wilderness are home to a large number of grizzly bears and other spectacular predators, has no permanent population of wolverines, just the occasional stray. Perhaps tourists are to blame, or perhaps the fact that, other than in national parks, wolverine trapping was legal in the United States until 2012. Not long after that *Wolverine Blog* post, also in March 2022, it was reported in the U.S. media that a wolverine had been found in Utah after killing or wounding eighteen sheep. Wolverines have been sighted eight times in Utah in the past fifty years, so this was a "once-in-a-lifetime event" according to wildlife researchers, who set up a trap baited with mutton. Despite the sheep killings, there was never any question of killing the wolverine; instead, after being trapped, it was fitted with a radio collar and released back into the wild. Rewilding initiatives are happening in many parts of the world; in Mongolia, for example, one ongoing project maps wolverines with a view to reintroducing them in their former territory.

The events of Douglas Chadwick's splendid *The Wolverine Way* also take place in Montana, and the tale of the wolverine dubbed M3, "Mr. Badass himself,"[27] and his mountaineering feats forms the literal high point of the book. Chadwick and his team followed wolverines over several years in the rugged, sometimes extreme mountains around Glacier National Park, in Montana and northward to British Columbia. Here, too, a handful of individuals roam across thousands of square miles and have no desire to be seen, since this has historically led to their being shot. Even so, and against all the odds, the scientists tracked and collared a few individuals and were also able to study their family relationships thanks to DNA analyses. They didn't fall for the temptation of assigning them human names, sticking to M for "male," F for "female," and combinations of numbers to indicate kinship.

M3 was the son of M23, a similarly sturdily built fellow, and the extremely fertile female F2, so the genetic odds were stacked in his favor, and he grew up to become a wolverine unlike any the world had seen before. His reputation preceded him, and when the scientists eventually managed to fit him with a radio collar, the rumors were not just confirmed but exceeded. He was so tremendously strong that it took a triple dose of tranquilizers to get the collar fitted. Despite this enormous dose, he soon returned to full strength, doing so in a quarter of the time it would have taken a regular wolverine to recover. He had left his father's home range in his early youth, roaming north into the territory of M6 and his son M18. M18 was observed with injuries from a fight and was ultimately driven out of his range, which M3 then took over—also laying claim to F15, the mother of F6, who soon became mother to M3's first son. After that, M3 extended his range to the north and made some enormously long journeys into Canada, as well as into other U.S. states. M3 feared no one; and perhaps he even feared nothing, because he was also responsible for probably the most spectacular feat of mountaineering ever performed by a wolverine. The signals from his radio collar bore witness to this journey.

M3 climbed to the top of Mount Cleveland, the highest peak in the national park at almost 10,500 feet. As if that weren't enough, he reached the summit via an almost impossible route: straight up a partly icy rock face. This was in January. It took him just ninety minutes to cover a vertical route with an elevation gain of nearly five thousand feet. This ascent, well beyond the abilities of any human, inspired a group of ardent mountaineers to attempt the same route to the summit; but despite crampons, ropes, and safety equipment, they had to give up. Quite apart from the sheer astonishment inspired by the knowledge that a wolverine is capable of this achievement, we are also left with a question: Why? He obviously wasn't seeking selfies, fame, or glory. Could this simply have been the fastest route to his destination? The GPS showed that he continued his journey across a razor-sharp ridge before descending and going farther westward across his vast territory. The wolverine barely seems to register topography. It chooses the shortest route between two points regardless of whether or not there's a peak in the way. In a week, it can cover inconceivable distances, often involving daily elevation gains of over 6,500 feet. The prosaic reason for this restless roaming is that it increases the chances of finding food, and the wolverine needs plenty of that to fuel its wanderings. It must also continually patrol the boundaries of its range, which it marks with scent to demonstrate its ownership rights.

It may also simply be that a wolverine, especially one in M3's league, has such an excess of energy and raw strength that it simply goes for it. According to Chadwick, several people have observed wolverines chasing grizzly bears away from prey. In other words, the wolverine—at least M3 and others of a similar caliber—appears to be fearless, because challenging a grizzly is hardly a walk in the park. Sometimes, it ends in death. The wolverine also has some physiological peculiarities: it has an oversized heart and remarkably large lungs, as well as an enormous thyroid gland, which might explain its reputation as an insatiable beast. With enough fuel in its tank, it can achieve feats that seem physiologically impossible.

But there is another possible explanation for this mountaineering activity, which Chadwick also discusses.

Perhaps a wolverine like M3 needs to challenge itself, push its limits, feel the sheer vital joy that comes from achieving a feat that is well-nigh impossible. It may even be that this feeling is intensified, as it is for us, when the climber gazes from the summit. While M3 may be the extreme mountain athlete of the wolverine world, it isn't unusual for these animals to climb peaks for no other reason than to reach the top. And that doesn't just apply to male wolverines either. F5, for example, climbed straight up the sheer sides of the monumental Bearhat Mountain in late winter. This mountain, which looks like an outsized and much steeper version of the Great Pyramid of Giza, is covered in ice and snow wherever they've managed to gain a foothold in its chinks and crevices, but is otherwise steep, black, and smooth. F5 climbed right to the summit, spent a while up there, and then went back down again. Why did she do this? It wasn't part of any route. Perhaps the simple answer was, as George Mallory famously said of Everest: because it was there. Chadwick laconically comments: "We have no better explanation than we have for why human mountaineers climb the tallest, hardest peaks."[28]

I like to think that, in its wolverine way, the wolverine is capable of feeling a similar sense of achievement and zest for life to us. Whatever the motivation, it is probably the same impulse that drives it up into the peaks of Jotunheimen, and perhaps the same impulse drives me too. The joy—mingled, at the steepest points, with terror—of reaching a summit via vertiginous routes is utterly irrational from a biological point of view. But then again, life isn't entirely rational, which is part of its charm. And perhaps the wolverine isn't a utility-maximizing *Gulo oeconomicus* focused solely on making rational choices that will enable it to eat, survive, and reproduce, but also fills its life with challenges and playful, life-affirming activities when it has enough energy to spare. Maybe it simply has a devil-may-care approach: life has to be about something beyond the daily struggle to fill your belly. I like that idea. We feel that, so why shouldn't they?

But are the lives of M3 and F5 better than those of the well-fed wolverines fenced in at the zoo? That depends on what we mean by *better*, and of course the wolverines in the zoo have no idea that there are others of their kind that possess magnificent primal strength and seem to live a richer life. Or lives that are, at any rate, more wolverine-ish; a life more attuned to their innermost being, the platonic ideal of the wolverine.

Not even the wolverine is totally invulnerable, though, and Chadwick also tells the tale of F21, M3's half sister—one of the many offspring of the productive F2. The team had managed to locate F2's den and fit her daughters, F21 and F22, with radio collars. The scientists maintained sporadic contact with mother and daughters as they roamed around the mountains over the summer, but in September, F21 was found dead. The six-month-old animal had lost her footing while traversing a steep cliff face in a snowstorm, fallen into the abyss, and died in a *bergschrund*, a cleft where the glacier meets the rock wall. Only with the utmost difficulty was the team able to rappel down to the dead wolverine, and they found claw marks in several places where F2 had tried in vain to climb down the precipice to her dead daughter before turning back to rejoin her surviving child, F22. The scientists tracked F2 and this daughter through the late winter, and saw that the pair interrupted their mountaineering activities with a hike to a cliff face beside a spectacular waterfall, where tracks in the snow showed that mother and daughter had stood shoulder to shoulder, apparently admiring the thundering cascade beneath them. We might ask what runs through a wolverine's mind.

The Ringebu Mountains don't offer anything remotely like the topographical challenges of Glacier's wild terrain, or even of Jotunheimen, for that matter, but the wolverine faces the same fundamental requirement if it is to survive here: finding enough food through the winter to fuel its tremendous metabolism, so it can roam for miles through the mountains and battle for territory and partners.

I've been lucky with the weather these past days, and it feels like the height of well-being to sit here on the dry heather leaning against warm smooth rock, eating my packed lunch, and watching the reindeer up there. This kind of experience is impossible to share, unless you happen to be sitting there with someone and assure each other how lovely it is. But that kind of sharing can also disrupt the sheer unfiltered contact between our sensory apparatus and our surroundings. A conversation would be an irksome interruption here. At the same time, it's nice to share unusual experiences there and then, not just after the event on social media; it creates a shared frame of reference, and in many ways it reinforces our impressions, but again I catch myself wondering about the difference between the autotelic and the heterotelic. When we and the wolverine climb peaks, is this something we do "just" for its own sake, making the activity itself the purpose, or is it simply a means to another end (which may be higher self-esteem, but also admiration or fame)? I think there are elements of both for both species. Feats of climbing have autotelic value as a form of mastery—what the philosopher and mountaineer Zapffe might have referred to as a "Dionysian affirmation of life." The fact that they may also give us a rush of reward hormones and higher self-esteem must almost be seen as an unintended heterotelic consequence. If the peak is simply a point en route to finding food or marking your territory, or producing subtly self-applauding selfies, books, or films, then Zapffe would demote it to a heterotelic means to an end.

In his characteristic way, Thoreau writes:

> But men labor under a mistake. The better part of the man is soon ploughed into the soil for compost. By a seeming fate, commonly called necessity, they are employed, as it says in an old book, laying up treasures which moth and rust will corrupt and thieves break through and steal. It is a fool's life, as they will find out when they get to the end of it, if not before.[29]

That sounds plausible enough until you remember that we can't take experiences of nature with us either, or at least not the ones that remain secret, locked into our own sensory apparatus. On the other hand, this marks the essential difference between the meaning *in* and the meaning *of* life. Our brief bursts of joy and love are the essence of life, and provide at least a kind of meaning in our lives that a joyless life does not have. Little rushes of reward hormones in the brain are the essence of utilitarianism, and I have no objection to such a reductionist way of perceiving things since it does nothing to diminish the fact that, lounging here in the heather, I feel the sun, I feel alive and surrounded by nature, and that makes me happy. I can both feel and think: *Yes, this is life,* but it'll stay trapped inside me unless I commit the heresy of committing it to print. Yet no text, whether objective or overblown, will be able to recreate my experience of this moment. It is impossible to convey a multifaceted, sometimes overwhelming, sensory impression in a one-dimensional text, which must then be interpreted by a recipient who requires the text to be translated into their own internal images. It's the same as with photos of the mountains: they're flat and bloodless by comparison with reality.

Again I think about the question of how nature can have value in the absence of a human observer. In both everyday speech and legislation, we refer with great certainty to the intrinsic value of nature, even though it's equally difficult to define both *intrinsic* and *nature.* Yet it undoubtedly does have a value, seen with a human gaze; most people would claim that nature enriches our existence, and not a few consider it to be crucial to our quality of life. That's certainly what I think, at any rate: a life without nature would not just be poorer, but poor, period. Qualitatively different, in other words. Perhaps this value of nature increases as more people see it. A kind of utilitarianism of nature. The value, the experiential value of nature certainly increases as it dwindles, as it becomes poorer in life and land area. The law of diminishing marginal utility applies here too. When that same nature is opened up, organized, and tamed for the maximum possible number of visitors, it loses many of its original qualities. No one has ever put this better than Zapffe: "Not enough people enjoy the thrilling solitude of Eagle Valley. Things will improve once we build a highway out there." Zapffe was also of the view that

> a mountain region with signposts is entirely different from a mountain region without them. It's like the difference between a virgin and a whore . . . when we visit the mountains, we do so to escape the world of calculations and money-grubbing and human infections in which we are forced to live, and not to re-encounter it in new variants or, heaven help us, in its all-too-familiar forms. We seek out undisturbed peace, which is the inalienable gift of the wilderness. That is why the first signpost is the disaster, not the twentieth or thirtieth.[30]

It's like an echo of Thoreau, only taken—if possible—to an even further extreme. And of course there's a certain elitism in this attitude too: the mountains should be off-limits to the general public, the common crowd, and accessible only to those who can master them. The wolverines of the human race.

Yet despite the fact that many feel a need to have the mountains to themselves or a select group of like-minded souls, they still have a clear compulsion to share their experiences through books, films, or social media. The need to convey extraordinary occurrences and achievements is apparently as old as our capacity for communication. An expedition that no one knows about can barely be said to have happened. Even Zapffe described his trips in detail, admittedly with a wit and irony that make it difficult to see this as a pose, but his descriptions nonetheless reflect a need to share. From the polar heroes like Nansen and Amundsen, Shackleton and Scott via later explorers like Helge Ingstad and Thor Heyerdahl to more modern nature explorers like Bear Grylls, documentation of the expedition and sometimes also of the experience of nature has been central and has also sometimes provided a livelihood. More prosaic camping trips through the Norwegian mountains are documented with handheld cameras, jerky footage of blisters, selfies, and blogs. And the compulsion to pose isn't exclusive to the male of the species, either, as evidenced by plentiful posts of young women in spectacular surroundings.

I see no need to dismiss this sniffily as bragging and posing; it may reflect a deeper need to show others both the landscape and our enthusiasm for it. We humans are social animals, after all. Good experiences and stories are made to be shared, which might make you wonder just how universal Thoreau's appreciation for solitary sylvan wandering is. It involves no heroic elements, since this is a gentle forest landscape, with villages and farms in the immediate vicinity. He meets people out here, receives visitors at his little cabin, and anglers come to fish at Walden. His walks in the forest are first and foremost an exercise in experiencing nature but above all a way of training his powers of observation, as well as his ability to see connections and understand the ecology of systems. Solitary wandering is crucial to this project, and to his ability to think great thoughts beneath the open sky—the thoughts that would otherwise be dispelled by the rush of daily life at ever-increasing speeds. But is *this* what life is all about?

Thoreau struck many a blow for loafing about—allowing oneself to be unuseful. And not just allowing oneself, but actually having "unusefulness" as a goal. It's a way of escaping the treadmill, the mill wheel of society, which tethers our thoughts and our sense of freedom with all its duties. But is unusefulness a meaningful way of life, even if idleness opens up the prospect of insight into both nature and ourselves? Doesn't that end up being a selfish escape that requires you only to lie in the grass and watch the clouds drift overhead as you experience inner well-being? Can this inner well-being constitute any kind of meaning over the long term? Now, Thoreau is cautious about using the word *meaning*; his clearest message is that the obligatory quest for usefulness is a distraction. It's quite possible that the best option is to do as Thoreau does: alternate. He goes to the village now and then to catch up with the local gossip (which he admittedly treats with a certain derision), and he has philosophical conversations with visitors to his little cabin, but he still spends most of his time communing with nature. For most people, though, gossip, the everyday trivialities, and their families *are* life itself, no matter how modest that may be and how little room it leaves for the cosmic perspectives. At worst, it may all boil down to "killing time" or inventing activities to keep us ticking over by making social connections. We "belong," we have life tasks (some even "meaningful"), morality ("an ethical YES and an ethical NO"), a kind of cultural development that, according to Zapffe, constitutes

> an ever-more elaborate palace, built from the sweat crystals the human soul excretes in its long, feverish battle with itself—caught as it is between the trivialities of self-preservation and magnificent, desperate destruction in fatal expansion, in a "union with everything" that excludes any possibility of choosing a suitable margarine brand.[31]

Or as Martin describes the same trivial matters in Ole Giæver's superb film *Out of Nature*: salmon on Fridays, or tacos if he's lucky. Martin also flees into nature to escape a dull, conventional existence and everyday trivialities.

Thoreau claims that "men have become the tools of their tools," and that "the mass of men lead lives of quiet desperation. What is called resignation is confirmed desperation."[32] This is also the point Yuval Noah Harari makes when he writes that we believed agriculture would free us, whereas it chained us instead to a repetitive annual cycle of food production. Our population grew, so more food was needed, then came the industrial revolution and the economy that further enslaved us to material goods and growth. All this being the opposite of the "Dionysian affirmation of life" out in nature, the wild, free, and "unuseful"—and freedom of thought. Still, we must ask ourselves whether Thoreau would have been satisfied with thought as an autotelic element if his ideas, his critique of civilization, indeed his plentiful advice for achieving a freer and richer life, had never found their way out of his own head. I don't believe he would. Thoreau was a former journalist, and his greatest joy was transforming thoughts into words; he loves lyrical turns of phrase and metaphors, refers to other people's scholarly works, and wishes others to read his. He wants to communicate and reach out, and that is why his reclusive existence is not entirely isolated. It has a purpose beyond his own spiritual enrichment.

A hermit-like existence is neither natural nor an ideal goal, not even for Thoreau: "I think that I love society as much as most, and am ready enough to fasten myself like a bloodsucker for the time to any full-blooded man that comes in my way. I am naturally no hermit."[33] No, none of us is, and it goes against every human's nature. We have been social animals since we became *Homo sapiens*. Yet it can still be good to be alone: solitude, and freedom from chatter, commotion, and claims on our time. Or it may be an escape from the deceptions and disappointments of society. I think we all benefit from time alone in nature; not just a half-hour run through the forest with a smartwatch measuring our pulse and earbuds filling our ears with music, but slow time when we simply *are*. I have this during my few stolen moments, islands in a sea of busyness, and I'd love to have more of them. They make life more joyous and therefore also give it a kind of meaning that complements the meaning I may feel on a good day when I have the sense that I've done something good and useful for my fellow humans and the future. And I don't think I have any compulsion to share this, either, or at any rate I never used to. Now I'm less certain, though, as I sit here thinking about whether I can convert my time and thoughts here in the mountains into text.

THE WIND HAS DROPPED, it's grown warm in the sunshine, and I assume that I must have sat here for a few hours on the lookout for wolverines and reindeer while my thoughts have flown with the falcons and the raven. I lie down and sleep for an hour in the heather. When the sun is low in the sky, I descend to the sparse birch forest again, unhook my backpack from the highest tree, and find two birches directly below that are a suitable distance apart, are sufficiently robust, and offer an unhindered view into the mountains on either side but are also sheltered from drafts. Here, I hang up a hammock, wondering whether or not to use a mosquito net as I do so. However, I've barely seen a single insect all day, and a mosquito net will rob me of a clear view of my surroundings and the stars, so I decide against it. Finding a suitable place to pitch a tent among roots and rocks is a challenge you're spared if you opt for a hammock. And when darkness falls, bringing its noises with it, you can switch on a flashlight to find out who's come to visit. I've often lain in a tent wondering who's padding and snuffling around outside.

I fire up the quick, light Primus stove, heat some water, and pour it into the pouch of freeze-dried food. Then I eat as twilight creeps up on me from the forest. There's still sunlight on the bare mountain behind me, so I take a hike to the top after finishing my food. On my way up, hardly a long stretch, I pass three sets of antlers, two of them pretty large, as well as a skull with both antlers still attached. Perhaps the skull is slaughter waste left by a hunter who already had a larger pair of antlers on the wall at home, but these other antlers are proof nonetheless that reindeer roam this area in the early winter when rutting season is over and the antlers, purpose served, are shed. It's actually ridiculously wasteful on the reindeer's part to produce new antlers every year, preferably larger than the last pair, especially as it requires large quantities of scarce minerals such as calcium and phosphorus, both of which are hard to come by in the barren bedrock here. The reason reindeer and other cervids treat themselves to such an apparently irrational extravagance is that this is the price they must pay to compete for status and females. It is the logic of sexual selection: expending the resources on other things would worsen the odds of success in the sexual marketplace. It's just like the song, colors, and sometimes extravagant mating rituals of birds. If nothing else, this demonstrates that a feel for the aesthetic is deeply embedded in nature.

Up on top, there's a cairn and a magnificent panoramic view, even though this is a modest mountain. I sit by the cairn and take out my binoculars. The snow on the Rondane Mountains is practically gone, and the evening light brings out each blue and distant ridge. It's a still August evening, and the only birds I've seen apart from the raptors are a handful of meadow pipits, which shyly hide away among the bushes, a wheatear, and a pair of silent redwings. All the zest for life and tireless territorial displays of the early summer have been replaced by a kind of sorry-for-being-here attitude. But there are sheep wherever I look, and the tinkling of their bells is audible throughout the mountains. As with so many things in life, these jingling bells can be too much of a good thing. And the sheep's constant gnawing at the vegetation must be affecting the ecosystem here. Still, they're exploiting unenclosed pastureland that would otherwise simply lie there "doing nothing"—it must be put to use. Any wolverine that happened by and nabbed a sheep here might be just as motivated by irritation at the bell ringing that has invaded the mountains as by hunger. And what about the sheep themselves? What's it like for them to have a bell around their necks that rings endlessly in their ears whenever they make the slightest movement?

On my way back down, I scare up a solitary male game bird and, as always, its cackle gives me a start. There's also a big round cairn down here, not as tall as the Bronze Age graves in the lowlands but with the same magnificent view. Could it really be that some chieftain among the wild reindeer hunters found his final resting place here one or two thousand years ago? I carry on down to the hammock, but once I get there, I realize I'm out of water. A creek or river runs a few hundred yards away, and I find myself thinking that the difference between a creek and a river is how easily it can be crossed. In this case, it's a big creek. There's sheep dung everywhere, and a herd of thirty cows, heifers, or oxen is ambling around farther upstream. I'm pretty dubious about the cleanliness of this mountain creek, but all the small springs have dried up, so I don't have any choice.

I have a sense of belonging in this forest of downy birch, the highest in the vicinity. As I gaze at the gentle, open landscape lit by the evening sun, with its grass, junipers, and scattered trees, it strikes me that its appeal may be rooted in our prehistory on the savanna. Some claim that the landscape of the savanna—open and easily surveyable but with the odd tree for shelter and flight, just like here—has left its evolutionary mark on us, so to speak. The birch forest is also pale, the trunks white at the base where they are covered with snow in winter, graying farther up at the level where witch's hair lichen dominates. The landscape will become different, darker if, or rather when, the spruce takes over. I lie in my hammock and watch a merlin "kiting" up by the mountainside; it hangs in the air, wings beating, then descends in an arc only to rise again and conduct a fresh survey. Many years ago, I found a merlin nest down here in the forest, and this too was noted down in my *Zoo Journal*, with a precise description of the spot so that I could find my way back to it the following spring in breeding season.

Then the last rays of the sun disappear, but once my eyes get used to the dark, the visibility is good well after the point at which, in an illuminated cabin, you'd say it was pitch-black outside. But here, too, the darkness comes at last, by which time I'm comfortably tucked into my sleeping bag. I've also brought along a proper sleeping pad, because the cold quickly seeps through the back of a thin sleeping bag. Two nights ago, we nearly had frost, and it isn't warm tonight either. I switch on my headlamp and pull out two books I brought with me because they were easy to carry. Two thin slivers. First, I leaf through Peder Cappelen's meditations on nature, *Alone With the Plateau*.[34] The word *alone* is essential here, although Cappelen doesn't make a big deal out of his solitary time in a simple mountain cabin from snow thaw to autumn. He's simply there, fishing, hiking, observing the wildlife, the wagtails' struggle to survive beneath the eaves, an outpost of existence for this delicate insect eater. The fox, the ptarmigan—the raven, like a prince of darkness on the rock face. I'd forgotten how poetic his language is, how fervent his feelings for nature, and how he lives the rich life by simple means without needing to analyze either himself or nature from the outside. Cappelen certainly bears rereading.

Next it's the turn of Kerstin Ekman's novel *The Wolf Run*.[35] The story centers on the encounter between aging Ulf Norrstig and a large wolf out in the forest of northern Sweden. Ulf has spent his life living from and with the forest, has hunted wolves, and has seen nature primarily as a place to be harvested. His meeting with the wolf opens his eyes to entirely new perspectives. As the great wolf comes into view between a juniper and a crooked pine on the edge of a bog, it strikes Ulf that this is *his* forest—the wolf's, that is. The wolf is naturally at home here, while humans are the invaders. "When I came to myself after the vision, I noticed how stiff and frozen I had grown from sitting still. How long it had lasted, I did not know. What I had experienced was beyond both time and any measure of it." The wolf, with its magnificent primal power, becomes a connection with a new side of nature. Nature *itself*, not just its instrumental value whereby animals are ranged on a spectrum from positive to negative, with none further out on the negative side than the wolf. And that takes us over into the realm of monsters. Even that great nature lover Linnaeus, Ekman's compatriot, proposed a plan for ridding Sweden of wolves in the eighteenth century. In his view, it was not just our right but our duty to manage nature in a way that was as beneficial as possible to humankind. The whole purpose of nature was to support our existence. Linnaeus's visions became reality two centuries later. In the 1960s, the wolf was declared extinct in Norway. Not until 1983 was a new wolf litter registered in Finnskogen, eastern Norway. DNA testing showed that the wolves originated from Finnish-Russian stock, a fact that has often been used to argue that they are not "truly" Norwegian and should therefore be regarded as intruders deserving of no rights. After being in the country since the Ice Age and then being hunted to extinction, the wolf is on the brink of becoming inbred. The wolverine was somewhat more successful in holding its own: a small residual population survived in the borderlands between the north of Norway and the north of Sweden. After it too gained a firmer footing in the late 1980s and scientists embarked on the process of genetic identification, there turned out to be a certain genetic difference between the eastern and western populations of wolverines, so a few western individuals must also have survived the persecution. Is it any wonder these animals are so shy?

I doubt whether Ulf's realization and conversion would have seemed credible in the 1960s; it certainly wouldn't have been believable in either the early 1900s or 1972. Nor even today—in Ulf's neck of the woods. Ulf's conversion into a friend of the wolf is seen as a betrayal.

This is a beautiful book, a quiet protest on behalf of a natural world that is shrinking before our very eyes, on behalf of the forest and the life that it contains. Perhaps it isn't just the wolf but also age and the reminder of his own mortality that make Ulf see nature with new eyes. Ekman, through Ulf, also sees how clear-cutting has transformed the forest from wilderness to plantation, to *the forest of death*. And it is a dry and blazing hot summer dominated by climate change. She knows both the forest and hunting culture. She is also able to describe the melancholy of aging in a way that resonates with me, tucked deep down in my sleeping bag.

I recall a summer job I once had thinning trees for one of the biggest forest owners in our district. Every morning, I would cycle seven miles or so with my lunch and axe in my backpack. I was alone in the woods the whole day, felling small pines and spruces that were between ten and thirteen feet tall. It's quicker to do this with an axe than a saw. I ate my packed lunch on a tree stump enjoying close encounters with the local wildlife. One day, a fox stopped by, another time a huge moose wandered straight past without even noticing me. Sitting there, motionless, I felt as if I'd blended in with the forest. After my job was finished in the late summer, a sinewy old chap with a horse and sledge came along and hauled the stripped trunks to the nearest road. When my period of employment ended, the forest owner, a well-to-do farmer, invited me to visit and offered me home-brewed ale in a traditional wooden bowl, served by his beautiful, blond daughter. Or that's the way I remember it at least. I was ushered into the farm's best parlor, which contained a colossal pine table and a huge cabinet decorated with traditional Norwegian rose painting. The farmer laid his paw of a hand on my shoulder and said I was a decent woodsman who would be heartily welcome to do more thinning work next summer. I didn't take him up on the offer. All those trees obstructed one crucial thing: the view. Peaceful as the forest may be, it doesn't offer the same sense of freedom as the mountains. So the following summer I applied for a job as a reindeer herder for the local *tamreinlag*, which I sadly failed to get, and ended up working as a glacier guide instead.

I read most of the book before switching off the light. Ulf, or Ekman, is no Thoreau. There's no philosophy of solitude here, no romantic notions, but rather a profound love of a nature that is on the wane. Given that so many people are able to describe nature in this way from very different starting points, there must be something deeper to what E. O. Wilson—the man who'd never seen a wolverine—called *biophilia*: an innate emotional attachment to all living things, chiseled out, as it were, by evolution. Biophilia is not a simple instinct, but what Wilson calls "a complex of learning rules." He thinks it should be seen as a potential that can be cultivated in different ways under the influence of culture. It can encompass everything from concern for the insect struggling for survival in a pond to the monumental oak tree, to the stand of trees, or the mountaintop—to the whole planet. One feature of biophilia as described by Wilson is that it is a fundamental human trait. It can assume different forms, it can be suppressed or nurtured through cultural impulses, but whatever the case, we have an innate need for contact with nature, an equally innate feeling for nature—and consequently, perhaps, an instinctive ethical response to nature. Truth to tell, I'm dubious about biophilia as an evolutionary trait, but biophilia in the sense of love of nature is an indisputable phenomenon.

A constantly growing body of research documents how nature, not just wilderness but small local woods too, helps lower our blood pressure and stress hormones while increasing our happiness and quality of life. Nature is more than just a pleasant, optional add-on. One interesting question is whether the sense of belonging we feel in nature can be reinforced by the realization of our evolutionary kinship with every living thing. The fact that we humans, like all organisms, form a continuous chain of life in the past, present, and future in more than a metaphorical sense should surely provide the basis for such a profoundly felt realization. It did, to some extent, for Darwin, and it does for Wilson. However, Linnaeus's profound feelings for nature did not spring from any sense of kinship with the life around him but rather from his faith in the magnificent creation God had placed on display for humankind. But that can also be a starting point for biophilia.

Biophilia's natural opposite is biophobia, and in many ways, we might expect that it would be easier to trace the latter than the former. After all, many of the aspects we originally appreciated about natural entities were related to consumption rather than to enjoyment and emotions, and there was little to be gained from feeling too much empathy for our prey. The wolverine and especially the wolf still evoke more biophobia than biophilia to this day. It is also possible that any potential to empathize with the animal per se is "switched off" when hunting; this is what Norwegian author and veterinarian Bergljot Børresen has referred to as "hunter insensitivity":

> Let us now imagine a group of humans from fifty thousand years ago. They are exactly like us in terms of capabilities, and live as hunters and gatherers. They see the animals and birds around them as autonomous "people," with feelings, language, customs, and knowledge as valid as their own. The hunters use this empathy—the positive social emotions—together with their experience and knowledge to predict where the prey can be found, and how it will behave during the hunt. But when the hunt itself begins, and the moment approaches when they will come into contact with and kill their prey, the hunters' empathy is interrupted. A state of mind takes over that modern hunters refer to as "the cold calmness."[36]

This capacity to kill in "cold blood" was also an evolutionary necessity. The problem today, according to Børresen, is that many of our dealings with animals are characterized by this same insensitivity. Yet empathy can still be evoked when we see *the other*, even in a wild animal, and suddenly recognize the animal's rights and intrinsic value—just as Ulf does with the wolf.

Once the light is out, I feel as if I'm surrounded by utter darkness. Six months ago, I stood in absolute whiteness not so far from here. Nor was it all that far from here that I saw the wolf cross my path. The darkness doesn't feel menacing to me; rationally speaking, there is absolutely nothing to be afraid of here other than the dark itself. Even so, I feel a flash of our forebears' fear of the night, from the days when there really was good cause to be afraid of the creatures out there that saw better than we did, had pointier teeth, and sharper claws. Back then, the darkness was a constant reminder of our vulnerability and how much we were at the mercy of nature. We felt the prey animal's fear at the watering hole and knew that death could come at any moment. Lying perfectly alone in the night, without walls or ceiling, affords us a glimpse of this humbling realization, even though, as I say, there is no longer any objective reason for fear. A safer place than where I am right now would be hard to find. It is also totally silent: no rushing waterfall, no soughing wind, no birdsong. It makes no difference whether my eyes are open or shut: I might just as well be lying deep inside a cave. After a few minutes, though, my eyes grow accustomed to the dark, and I can make out the contours of the branches above me, and the pale antlers I have placed beside the tree at the foot of my hammock. It is still too early in August for a full starry sky. Quite when I slip off to sleep I don't know, but I must have slept, because I suddenly wake up with a start.

And what wakes me is a scream—I believe. At first I think it may have been a dream. Then comes another scream from the darkness, short but loud. Then silence. I lie for a long time listening but there's no more. It's impossible to identify the screamer. It could have been a grebe, but it sounded a bit too loud for that, and besides there's no lake in the vicinity. It may have been a cervid, a hare in its death throes, the combined bark-and-howl of a fox, or it may have been a lynx, but hardly a wolverine. The wolverine's repertoire of sounds consists of snarls and hisses. The only thing I'm certain of is that it isn't dangerous. But even so, the hairs on the back of my neck rose, and it's a while before sleep returns. The moon has come out, a low, yellow full moon that shines bashfully as it passes behind the birches. I lie awake until it sinks like an ember in the west, and I listen out, but it is perfectly quiet.

Early next morning, a bit chilly and stiff, I lie for a while listening as I wait for the warmth of the sun. I hear some birdsong, though it's a pale imitation of the early summer orchestra. A flock of thrushes hunts for blueberries on the south-facing hillside. They'll hold out here for a few more months, staining the first snowfall with semi-digested berries before seeking lower ground and, eventually, southern climes. Few birds have actually left the mountains yet; they're just not much in evidence, with the exception of the noisy fieldfare, that is, although it too is noticeably quieter. Finches and tits flutter around cautiously, harvesting the summer's seeds and fruits and maintaining contact with each other in bashful fluting tones. Only the frailest insect eaters, the warblers, are already feeling restless this early in August. The first frosty night reveals the gravity of the situation: the food is disappearing fast. The willow warbler, whose song I consider the theme tune of summer, is silent, preparing for its migration to tropical Africa—if it isn't already on its way. The reason why it opts to make the long and perilous journey back to barren highland Norway is simply that these highlands aren't as barren as we tend to think. The short summer offers more food with less competition and fewer enemies than in Africa, where they would be more ruthlessly subject to the law of the jungle. The difference is big enough to make the journey worthwhile. The most impressive migratory bird is the Arctic tern, which breeds in Svalbard. From there, it migrates each year to the opposite pole, where it finds food amid the drift ice during the Antarctic summer before embarking on the return journey to just below the North Pole.

I boil up some more coffee, eat three slices of bread—alternating the toppings in my customary order: cheese, then salami, then brown goat's cheese—eat a handful of cloudberries scattered with sugar, pack my sleeping bag, sleeping pad, and hammock, and I'm ready. The sun hasn't managed to force its way through the clouds today, but the temperature is rising. For the first time in my life, I feel a twinge in my knee and have to tread carefully. It's nothing in the scheme of things, of course, but I take it as a warning. August, yes: old age. I follow the Breia down, catch two trout in the pool using a spinner, drop by the cabin, and do a quick circuit of the small lower-lying bogs by the rough-legged buzzards' cliff. The frost has taken its toll here too. All I find is four cloudberries, snugly sheltered beneath the skirts of the spruces on the edge of the bog. There are no birds on the cliff other than a great spotted woodpecker that swoops down from a dried spruce and lands in a birch on the other side of the bog. Two tits flutter among the trees, but otherwise late summer silence reigns. I fry the fish and guzzle a pound of cloudberries for dessert. Once again, I lock up the cabin and head home.

The cornfields are yellow down in Gudbrandsdalen and the second silage cut is underway. I stop off at Mum's en route, and together we go to the cemetery to plant flowers on the grave where Marit and Dad lie side by side. I see now that the map lichen on the stone has faded after all. Mum kisses the gravestones as she always does, and whispers to Marit and Dad that she misses them, and that they must rest in peace. Then she tells Dad she'll be joining him soon.

I travel onward in a mournful frame of mind. The late summer heat fills the lowlands, and it's a scorching day of radiant sunshine, but my minor-key mood is exacerbated by the melancholy I always feel on leaving the mountains, as I pass through ever-tamer landscapes, past more and grayer buildings, and in the end see only remnants of nature crammed between roads and buildings. At one of the busiest crossroads, a family of eight to ten spruces stand around consoling each other on a tiny scrap of green squeezed between three intersecting roads. The transition is worst in winter, when the sunlit snow of the mountains stands in stark contrast to the gray slush of the city. However, I have chosen to live my life as a useful member of society here in the city, so I have no choice. There is so much to be done. And this is where my social life is. The mild feeling of depression, of loss, and longing lasts until the busyness takes over and absorbs all my mental capacity. At the same time, I'm uncertain whether the intense sense of *living* would remain after several weeks or months in the mountains; they too can be dismal in times of rain, slush, and November darkness.

Love of nature is probably the same as any other love: the fervor gradually abates, regaining intensity after an absence. But it will never vanish altogether, whereas the love in a couple relationship may well do so. Of course, love can blossom and endure if we cultivate it consciously. And perhaps love of nature will grow over time if we are simply in it and give ourselves up to it. I have no way of knowing this, because I've never tried it—a year alone in nature, that is.

I'VE NEVER BELIEVED in fate. Random events are just that: random. Even so, they sometimes feel *almost* miraculous. Shortly after my return, my son Knut sends a message asking if I can guess what he met on his way into the mountain forest in Østerdalen, a few dozen miles east of the spot where I camped. They came face-to-face on an agricultural road in the sparse highland pine forest that's only open in the summer, at a distance of just ten to fifteen yards. For two seconds, they made eye contact, the wolverine and he, before it turned in its tracks and sauntered off through the pine forest. A magical moment. Lucky Knut. His encounter inspires me to take a new trip, this time to the proper mountains. The Ringebu Mountains are a pleasant enough place to roam, but when I stand on their rounded peaks and look north to Rondane and especially northwest to Jotunheimen, I always feel the pull of those peaks and gorges. Those are the *real* mountains. So a bit later in August, I succumb to the pull and seek out the highlands, returning to the neighborhood of Wolverine Peak, where I truly feel at home.

I HAVE TWO possible hikes in mind. Into Leirdalen, camping by the lake, Leirungstjønnin, then down into Svartdalen the following morning and maybe up toward the truly Alpine peaks of Knutsholstind or Tjørnholstind. A taste of the highlands and also a chance to scout the fields of snow for tracks. But the weather forecast is looking changeable, so tents and precipices aren't appealing. I choose the other, gentler option: Nautgardstind, where wolverine tracks were seen in a snowdrift on the southern side just two days ago, according to "reliable sources." Besides, this is another mountain that deserves to be revisited, almost fifty years after my childhood friend Kjetil and I were up there and named it Wolverine Peak. Very few people hike in this area, or at least not the last leg of the ascent; the first part, by contrast, is one of the freeways of the Jotunheimen Mountains.

It's already late morning by the time I set off from Bessheim Mountain Lodge, so I hike quickly up the broad path to the alpine lake, Bessvatn, following the river with its many small waterfalls and pools. Bessvatn is among the world's clearest lakes, by the way; on one occasion, I brought some gear up here and measured the light penetration to the depths of this lake myself. When I reach the lake's outlet, I take the right-hand fork of the path, which eventually runs down the mountainside to another lake, Russvatn. Immediately after the point where the path forks, there are two shallow fishless tarns—one of the remaining places where the "primal shrimp," the fairy shrimp, still swims its graceful backstroke. Down toward Russvatn, a broad path continues through the sparse birch forest. It's hot and I've been moving quickly, so I stop for a quick dip in the icy water, mostly tempted by the beautiful sandy beach.

Afterward, I walk along the northern edge of Russvatn, a beautiful long lake that stretches like a crescent moon around the northern side of Besshø mountain until it meets the ridge, Besseggen. The lake is surrounded by peaks that are all more than 7,200 feet high. As if by a quirk of fate, Nautgardstind to the north is exactly the same height as Besshø to the south—7,408 feet. My first hike up Besshø was also my first and only close encounter with a golden eagle, and that, too, happened a good many years ago now. As I rounded the summit from the northern side one early morning, the eagle took off from directly behind the cairn and soared off over Lake Gjende on mighty wings, brown wing feathers shining in the morning sun. Directly opposite the spot where I am walking, due west of me, lies the mighty peak of Surtningssui, a gentle giant of 7,769 feet.

After walking along the lake for a while, I head upward to start on the hike to the top. Nautgardstind is a formidable pile of gravel to my north, and, as mountain hikes go, it's unchallenging except for the endless scree formed of rocks in varying sizes. But like so many of the mountains around here, it has at least two faces, and its northern side certainly lives up to the designation of *peak*: here, smooth rock plummets down to cirques and glaciers. From the south side it's accessible from all angles, but I'm sick of scrambling through scree, so I aim for some fields of snow a bit farther over on the mountainside, which seem to extend to the summit almost without interruption.

From afar, I spy a small herd of twelve to fifteen reindeer descending the snow-covered mountainside in my direction. These reindeer are just barely tame and enjoy an optimal existence compared with most other livestock, living a free life out in the mountains on their own reindeer terms. True, they are subject to ear tags and slaughtering season in the fall, but at least they are spared a degrading indoor life in semi-darkness, in cramped cubicles, robbed of almost everything that makes life worth living. The animals clearly haven't noticed me yet, and only when I reach the lower edge of the large snowdrift do they stop in vague confusion. I see now that this snowdrift really does stretch almost all the way to the top, and I'm already looking forward to the descent. To give the reindeer time to think things over and consider a strategic retreat, I stop for a while until, with some reluctance, they start to move back upward. There are two calves in the herd, one of which is an albino—perfectly camouflaged against the white snow, but quite the reverse on the scree slope. I walk slowly after them, assuming they'll soon veer off to the side; but they, like me, clearly find it more enjoyable to walk on snow than stones. The sun has softened the uppermost part, but these layers of eternal snow are always hard beneath, offering firm footing for both humans and reindeer. The reindeer are still unwilling to move out into the scree. Now and then they stop to check whether I'm following. I am, and since time's getting on, I can't take it *too* easy if I want to get to the summit and back again before nightfall. It's no longer midsummer and now, in the latter half of August, the nights have become properly dark again. In the end, the little herd stops and lets me come pretty close before drifting out into the scree and allowing me to pass at a safe distance.

It's an endless hill, this one, and even after the snow peters out up there, a long stretch still awaits me, coarse scree all the way to the top. I walk on the edge of the snowdrift looking out for any exciting items that might have been revealed by the thaw. These snowdrifts may have been here as long as several thousand years, but now they are melting rapidly, and from time to time they throw up some almost miraculously well-preserved artifacts: skis, clothes, shoes (the oldest dating back more than three thousand years), and hunting weapons belonging to people who traveled up here for one reason or another in some far-off era.

I find nothing of interest until I'm right at the top of the snowy mountainside. Here, I see a track that enters the field of snow from the right-hand side, leaves impressions in the snow for some twenty yards, and then vanishes into the scree to the left. My pulse, already pretty high after ascending a tough slope close to seven thousand feet above sea level, climbs even higher. *Wolverine*. It feels totally unreal, and almost like running into the animal itself. So, it *is* here. It has left a sharp impression on the wet snow, which has barely begun to melt at the edges, and the claw marks are clear. It walked here today, perhaps in the early hours of the morning, maybe just now. If it had passed by twenty yards higher up, it would have walked only through the scree and I wouldn't have had a clue it had been here at all. I *could*, of course, consider it bad luck that I wasn't here earlier or the wolverine later, which would have allowed me a glimpse of the legendary creature. But few of us think that way. First of all, even over a period of just twenty-four hours, the odds are overwhelmingly *against* my being here at the same time as a wolverine.

Let's say it could have been within my field of vision for a maximum of six minutes; that means I would have had a 10 percent probability of seeing it within the space of a single hour, and the probability of seeing it within a space of twenty-four hours would have been 0.4 percent. Strictly speaking, less, since it would have been too dark to either hike or see the animal here for several of those hours. But we humans are rarely disheartened by poor odds and generally have an impressive ability to see the positive in life. How lucky that I broke my left arm and not my right one, even though the probability of suffering the fracture was far lower than 0.4 percent to start off with. I feel lucky to have seen this track, and the likelihood of *not* coming across it was staggeringly higher.

I measure the prints and find that the biggest impressions are roughly six inches. It was a large male that passed this way, and his range encompasses many high peaks. Maybe he has patrolled them all. I follow the sight line marked by the dead-straight prints. It points directly toward a striking depression between two peaks. From there, perhaps the wolverine did a circuit south, and he may already have crossed the valley of Veodalen. Could he be on his way to his stomping ground by Wolverine Peak? That would be an easy hike for a wolverine: a male can easily cover fifty miles in a single night. It may also be that he has found a coarse talus slope down here where he is spending the day, maybe with the delicious scent of reindeer in his nostrils. A bit farther on I see a knoll protruding from the scree, so I run over there and sit down on it with my binoculars. There are several snowy slopes and snowdrifts in this area, and I scour them all in the hopes of seeing a black mustelid bounding along against the white backdrop. There's nothing to see, though, not even any tracks. Even so, I can almost feel its presence, and it is quite possible that it can see me right now.

Exhilarated, I hike the last, tough leg to the summit where the bedrock emerges from the mass of scree, and a modest cairn has been built on the base of fractured rock. Russvatn and Besshø lie to my south, and a sheer drop to the glacier, Nautgardsbreen, to my north. Like many of the glaciers here, this one has retreated over the past decades. The summit is flanked by two other connected peaks. I see peak after peak, most of which I have climbed thanks to my youthful mania for collection, which at one point focused on summits. And it all started here on Nautgardstind. I have no recollection of the actual summit from that first mountain hike, only the overwhelming impression of the surrounding mountains that I was taking in for the first time back then. The peaks I specifically remember are the ones that were genuinely difficult to scale.

This is the second time I've been here, and I'll probably never return. Not because I won't be able to hike here, but because I won't have any reason to. There's a last time for everything, and there's nothing melancholy about the thought that this is my final farewell to the view from Nautgardstind, precisely because I know that I *can* come here again if I want to—and because there are other summits I want to sit on. If this were the last time I could climb a real mountain, the thought would be unbearable. Yet that day will also come.

Suddenly I realize it's very late in the day, and not long afterward I hear thunder in the distance. A mountaintop is no place to be when there's lightning, so I quickly head back toward the snowdrift. Running and sliding down on the snow, I've almost made my way back down by the time the rain catches up with me. On my way up, I'd noticed a flat slab of rock that formed a roof over an outcrop, and that's where I seek shelter. The thunder rolls around the mountains with a mighty echo and the lightning illuminates the mountainsides at regular intervals. Someplace down toward Russvatn I spy a sharp green field of vegetation. A spring rises here, rich in phosphates and other minerals from the depths of the earth. I creep as far in toward the rock face behind me as I can to escape the pouring rain, which will probably pass if I can hold out for half an hour. I don't have much of a choice. What's the wolverine up to now? Probably roaming onward, impervious to the weather, on its way to wherever, for whatever reason, it has decided to go. A downpour like this is barely worthy of the animal's attention, whereas bitter experience has taught me how cold we humans can get from a soaking in the mountains. Everything stiffens, thoughts and reactions alike.

I'm probably not the first person to have taken refuge here, and to pass the time, I poke about in the vegetation, move around the rocks, and dig up a bit of the scant soil with a flat stone. Two small sharp fragments of stone catch my eye, and when I wash them—by briefly holding my arm out beyond the sheltering slab—they prove to be unmistakably flint. Not arrowheads, but sharp nonetheless; small fragments that can only have gotten here because someone once sat in this spot and knapped their stone tools or struck a spark for a fire. Perhaps they were preparing for a reindeer hunt the next day. It isn't such a surprising find, really: there have always been people in the mountains, every trail has been traveled, and most such slabs have at some point provided shelter for people with some business out in the mountains. But did these mountain folk go all the way to the summit? And if they did so, did they have any goal other than scouting for reindeer? Did they once sit on the summit of Nautgardstind and think how magnificent and beautiful it was in some inexplicable way, or did they just see the mountains as barren regions they only sought out to help their own little flock keep body and soul together? As I pointed out earlier, "Nasty Peak" is a pretty common name even for mountains that we consider beautiful; and Surtningssui, meaning "Black Sow," is hardly a flattering name either. How did we even come up with the idea that mountains are *beautiful*? After all, they're the very negation of life: rocks, ice and snow, cold, and danger. Perhaps that's precisely it, though: the mountain is the one remaining pillar of wildness and peril in a tamed life that can sometimes make us feel we live in a safety-addicted society, subjugated through a kind of systemic lobotomization that has led us to voluntarily fence ourselves in.

I believe that the hunters of bygone days did hike up to the summit, that they liked the view and weren't just there to scout for reindeer from a higher vantage point. I believe they sat by their campfire when the weather was good and told lively tales, recounted scenes from previous hunts, and planned the next one. They faced hunger and sudden death, but that was just part of life. I believe they lived free and happy lives here before becoming enslaved by production. The last person who held these flint shards was a hunter from another age, but the mountains were the same, and their dreams and yearnings were probably much like my own.

The rain eases off after just twenty minutes and I hurry onward. The first hint of twilight has already started to settle over the landscape even though it has cleared up, and a chillier fall wind is tangible in the air. I take the fastest route down to Russvatn and follow the shore, a kind of roller coaster of small sandy ridges shot through with creeks. Now and again, there are sandy beaches, and in a couple of places there are some very inviting camping spots. I should of course have brought my tent along on such a long hike, but there's no point dwelling on that. By the time I'm back at the outlet of the lake, it's pretty dark, but the last remaining light from the evening sky is mirrored in the water, casting a magical glimmer across it. I continue, gradually registering that I've been on the move for a long time; but when I'm in the flow, as now, I can hike like this for several more hours if need be, even though I know I'll pay for it the next day. Up on the ridge by the fairy shrimps' lake, I suddenly start at the sight of large animals dashing away from the path. I catch a glimpse of antlers against the night sky—reindeer. I pass quite close by, hearing the nervous tramping and snorting of the animals out there in the darkness. The last part of the hike goes slowly, but the path is paler where the vegetation has been worn away, so it's possible to find my footing even though I'm walled in by darkness. One careful step at a time, I make my way down into the birch forest at last, and I'm back at Bessheim half an hour after midnight. After twelve hours on the go, I'm pretty done in, so I call it a night at Bessheim Mountain Lodge.

Autumn

I'VE LONG BEEN planning an excursion in this area. Kjetil and I have discussed a fiftieth-anniversary hike to mark that trailblazing trip of ours through the mountains with bivouac bags, homemade cooking utensils, rolled oats, and a job lot of water-damaged canned fish cakes. We've earmarked enough time to hike some parts of the route again in mid-September, a season when the mountains can be at their most beautiful but winter is ready to seize control. Once again, several wolverine sightings have been reported in the area, and local sheep farmers are in despair over the ravages of these predators. We've mulled taking in a couple of peaks along the way too, but it's as windy as it has been throughout the summer. Every single mountain hike between February and August has been blighted by bitter winds with only brief interludes of calm, and the weather forecast for this weekend is for sleet and wind speeds of forty-five miles per hour in precisely the spot where we're planning to camp, so we have to opt for a stopgap solution. Over the years, we've gone on a good many hikes together, although they've been fewer and shorter than we dreamed of back then on the summit of Nautgardstind. On some hikes, we've had plenty of company, other times, it's just been the two of us. Hiking in a group changes the dynamic, offering more laughter and more stories and more competition, but although you may experience just as much nature, you have less opportunity to become absorbed in it. We have bagged peaks aplenty with youthful arrogance, but it now strikes us both how much more dangerous the mountains have come to seem with the passing years. We see the risk of rockfalls in places where the thought would never have dawned on us a few decades ago. Once again, it's that paradoxical fact: when we are young and have everything to lose we do not fear sudden death in the mountains, only dying of old age. That's why it no longer feels like a searing defeat to end up at the cabin in the Ringebu Mountains instead. Fifty years ago, this would have been intolerable, but now we console ourselves with the beautiful fall colors as we ramble through the gentle terrain, gazing in toward the peaks of Jotunheimen and Rondane.

And the colors really are at their most intense: the blueberry bushes are red, their berries big and juicy. The first night frost has yet to come. The blueberry shares this space with crowberry bushes, also laden with berries, although their foliage insists on remaining green all year round. The dwarf birch displays every color on the spectrum from green to shades of orange and red, then dark red and brown. The downy birches are decked in yellow hues, but it's a different yellow from the willows that line the bogs and creek beds. Somewhat higher up there are three clusters of small downy birches, one of which is yellow, the second orange, and the third bright red. The genetic variants also express themselves in the pigments. Sedge and grass form a pale yellow carpet. The mountaintops themselves loom up like red and orange pyramids, decked in dwarf birch and heather all the way up to the point where scree and map lichen take over. Closer to the summit, chalk-white fields of star-tipped cup lichen and reindeer lichen surround patches of green crowberry and bearberry. Both species yield rather bland berries, but what bearberries lack in flavor they make up for in the color of their foliage, which ranges from purple to a truly extraordinary red, the most intense of all the fall colors in the mountains. In between lie small clusters of dwarf willow in modest yellow. We are between the peaks of Øverlihøgda and Veslefjell, on our way into the dip. Higher up we come across some of these patches of bearberry surrounded by white heather in between largish rocks covered in the intricate green patterning of map lichen.

These are the colors of decay, the green and orange carotenoids and the red anthocyanins, but why do we find them so beautiful? Everyone sees it that way, and all emotions that are universally human must necessarily have a deep evolutionary basis. Could it simply be that a signal coded deep within our primate brains tells us that red and yellow signify ripe fruit and berries? Precisely the food that was most important to our distant ancestors long before we parted ways with the chimpanzees' forebears five million years ago. I can't think of a better rational explanation, but so much about our relationship with mountains is irrational—like this business of seeking out summits, ice, and snow that offer us nothing but toil and danger. Well, they're beautiful all the same, we tell each other, the way all hillwalkers do at this time of year if they have anyone to share the experience with. Only a bit later does the fall melancholy take hold. When the color pigments break down and only shades of brown remain. When fungus lays a gray veil over the remaining leaves, which also acquire the liver spots of old age—black patches of tar spot fungus—before falling off the trees. In a month, the downy birches' naked branches will bristle against a gray sky, with only vestiges of leaves and colors here and there; the blueberry bushes will have given up the ghost and dropped their leaves, focusing now on the buds that will form the next generation of leaves in spring. Only the bearberries stubbornly retain some of their color. A sadness lies over the mountains in these late fall days, a sadness that will persist until the snow lights up the landscape once again.

But for now, it's beautiful. A light rain-shower that intensifies the colors is succeeded by sunshine, and we eat a packed lunch in the middle of a field of bearberries and star-tipped cup lichen, sheltering from the wind behind a hillock and feeling grateful that we can still hike for hours in the mountains fifty years on. At the same time, we know it can't last: friends are starting to have health problems, we mostly talk about the hikes we've already taken, discuss not our own careers but those of our children—and the steepest peaks no longer hold the appeal they once did. But the sun warms us, and life is good to live in the here and now; after a while, we begin, somewhat overconfidently, to discuss new plans, routes, and hikes we'll take in Jotunheimen in the summer.

We press on. A ptarmigan flies up from the bearberry bushes, its wings white but its back still brown. It is followed at once by two more. Well within shooting range, thinks the hunter in me, and we are able to follow them for a good while before they round a hill. I catch myself instinctively reaching for my rifle but am glad I don't have it with me. I'd only have felt guilty about contributing to the further decimation of an already meager population. Yet another ptarmigan flies up, its unmistakable gargling cry identifying it as a cock. It's hunting season, and a reindeer hunter and ptarmigan hunter who passed through Borkebua the previous day have written terse entries in the cabin visitors' book. Both mention their poor haul. No one has seen any reindeer in this neck of the woods, the reindeer hunter writes, while the ptarmigan hunter has bagged just one of the paltry three ptarmigans he saw. That's bad news for anyone keen on tracking wolverines, because for all its roaming, this perpetual motion machine preys first and foremost on reindeer. And when there are no ptarmigans to be had either, that means even emergency rations are scarce.

In previous years, I might have found snow hollows left by flocks of twenty to thirty ptarmigans around here; sometimes I'd come upon even larger flocks of chalk-white rock ptarmigans. You could get right up close to them early in the fall, although they became increasingly shy as the flocks sought each other out in late fall and winter. I used to hunt here, but I gave it up many years ago when it got so you'd see more bird dogs than birds on a daylong hike. My great-grandfather came from a smallholding in the local village of Ringebu, but since it didn't yield enough food for all the children, he grew up in Sollia, a small community some thirty miles north, apparently in the home of childless relatives. I have a vague recollection of him as a pipe-smoking old man with a great shock of hair. He came from an era when life was a matter of the profoundest gravity. An era when hunting was not a hobby but necessary for your survival. When I was due to go on my first hunting trip, my grandfather gave me a photo that showed the result of a weekend's hunting around here between the First and Second World Wars. Two men stand holding a ladder whose length is hung with ptarmigan, interspersed with the occasional black grouse or hare. Again: a handful of people out in endless nature. Two generations on, the situation is reversed.

From Borkebua, we hike up to Gråhøgda. Here, too, a male bird takes flight, a rock ptarmigan cock, its cry slightly higher pitched than that of the willow ptarmigan. The Breitjønn tarns glitter to the north. On our way back we pass by the great raptor mound, the result of thousands of years of carcass stripping and fertilizing by many different birds of prey. Now, in fact, a bird is sitting right there on the lower side, a big gray falcon—so big that it just has to be the rare gyrfalcon, loathed by hunters as a competitor for ptarmigans but protected now after being hunted to the brink of extinction. We get pretty close up before it takes off, and I'm excited to see whether there's any prey there, but there's nothing to be found. It's a bad year for ptarmigans throughout southeastern Norway, so life is tough for the gyrfalcon, despite its protected status. Beside the big cairn on Øverlihøgda, a tattered bivouac bag flutters in the wind. I look at the leather tag attached to the bag with an eyelet: *Jervenduk*, wolverine tarp, it says above a logo of a wolverine. And that's the closest we get to the animal today. Why is a bivouac bag lying out here like a silent witness to some drama in the mountains? Answer comes there none, but no one is willingly parted from their bivouac bag.

Farther down, we cross the upper mountain forest and scare up a solitary reindeer buck, which vanishes in the direction of Veslefjell. It's unusual to meet lone reindeer like this one, although it does happen. Is he a dethroned alpha male roaming around in bitter isolation? Is he a cunning chap who knows that the reindeer hunting season is underway and that his best bet is to hide away alone down here in the woods until winter comes and it's safe to rejoin the herd—or is he a Thoreau of the reindeer world who thinks life out here in the mountains is best lived in solitude?

Twilight has descended by the time we return to the cabin. We have hiked for seven hours and are pleased to find that the machinery of our bodies still seems to be in good working order. After lighting the stove, we sit around reminiscing and laughing, almost like in the old days. Back then, the decades to come lay before us like an eternal shield against old age. Now, that eternity of time lies behind us and there is no longer any consoling buffer, yet life still isn't so terrible.

Next day we head farther into the mountains. The whole road is lined with cars and camper vans, and red hunting caps and hounds are visible on the plateaus. We set off from Friisbua, one of the two small stone cabins Professor Jens Andreas Friis had built to serve as shelters for hunters and anglers. Friis undoubtedly had a certain spiritual kinship with his contemporary, Thoreau, although he was more interested in the mountains than the forest and, above all, in harvesting from the mountains. Yet he writes in romantic terms about the blessings of freedom and the joy of solitude in the mountains; even more romantically, in the spirit of Rousseau, he speaks of the primitive yet free and natural life of the Sami people. His *Into the Mountains in the Vacations, or Hunting and Angling Life in the Highlands* starts with a poetic exhortation extending over several pages that urges readers to experience this health and freedom at least once: "Up there, you will gradually come to feel how the dust and rust of worldly life that has settled heavily upon your soul bit by bit is gradually brushed off and washed away... Come, then, and journey, all ye who can escape the oppressive City Air and the constricted Views."[37] What a life Friis must have led in these mountains.

We take a breather behind a hillock, once more amid the star-tipped cup lichen, bearberries, and map lichen, with a view of Friisvannet Lake shimmering silver down below, then the local heights and valleys, and beyond that again, blue mountains and dancing clouds. In fifteen years, this will no longer be an easy hike for us, but it is for now. If that time comes, it will be a victory for us to get up here. It's those shifting baselines again—a blessing when it comes to adjusting our expectations about mountain hikes or our own reflections, but a dangerous adaptation when five ptarmigans on a daylong hike seem like a lot, or when we get used to increasingly unpredictable snowfall in winter. Eighty-five-year-olds in the ski tracks—bent-kneed, stooping, and moving in slow motion—are well aware that they can't ski as fast as they used to, but at the same time, they know that they can ski faster and farther than almost all their contemporaries; indeed the mere fact of skiing at all is a feat that gives a kind of meaning to life. Without either of us saying so, we both know that only a limited number of mountain hikes remain ahead of us, and as the years go by, the likelihood grows that *this* one will be the last.

We wander into the mountains on the eastern side with a view of ridge after blue ridge stretching in toward the highest peaks of the Rondane Mountains, all topped by the fall's first scattering of icing sugar. Winter is coming and fall is the skier's spring. The next time I'm here, there will be snow for tracking and maybe even decent skiing conditions. It will be white, pure, and virginal. There will be hare tracks in the willow thickets that protrude from the snow, willow ptarmigan tracks embroidering the river valleys, rock ptarmigan tracks around the summits. A heavy moose may struggle its way through the snow, grazing on the willow before it heads down into the winter forest for good. And then, in the low pre-Christmas sun, right before the blue hour perhaps, a purposeful wolverine track will lead into the mountains, heading for the reindeer that have now found their winter grazing grounds near Storkvien, where the wind has blown the ridges bare. I picture it all and cannot wait.

Year's End

IT IS FAR FROM TRUE that nature is always fabulous, not even in the mountains. Rigidly insisting that it's "a nice day" out when all the signs indicate the contrary is simply annoying. Interpreting cold and wet as "brisk" whatever the circumstances does no one any favors, and is reminiscent of the phony adjectives so liberally applied by real estate agents. Yet it is surprising how often nature proves generous, even when the view outside a cottage window looks distinctly unappealing. I have never returned from a hike without feeling some positive effect, some improvement in my state of mind—sometimes even euphoria; you can walk your way out of the darkest mood and return with a brighter outlook on life. It's almost like the baloney those lifestyle gurus spout about seeing the possibilities rather than the problems. It isn't always possible to pull ourselves up out of the mire by our own hair as Baron Munchausen did, but nature really is one big happy pill—with no prescription, no side effects, and no price tag. I've often thought that life can never be entirely empty while we have nature. If I lost everything—family, friends, job—I'm not certain that nature could save me from the abyss, but if I had anything left, I would also still have nature and its sunbeams, no matter how tough life got. Thoreau has of course had that very same experience: "There can be no very black melancholy to him who lives in the midst of Nature and has his senses still."[38] When my sister Marit died suddenly and unexpectedly aged twenty-one—at precisely the age when life should be in full bloom—nature was what saved me and gave me enough breathing space to try and keep my parents' zest for life alive, but part of them died with Marit. They never recovered the life they once had, only enjoying the occasional glimmer of happiness that was soon clouded over. It became an obsession with me to do things that might bring them joy, to give them grandchildren. The quest to find a worthy gravestone among the many candidates on the plateaus of the Ringebu Mountains was a curiously painful yet beautiful experience. There's much I've forgotten, but I do remember that. Dad's gray face, contorted by the pain of existence, yet still alive to the mountains. Mum's dead gaze, which flickered briefly into life when she gave the stone her seal of approval, and we knew that Marit would be able to lie beneath a piece of the mountain.

I have turned to nature and the mountains in times both good and bad; they have brought substance and joy to my life. And a feeling of belonging in the cosmos, insofar as a rational non-pantheist like me is capable of that. That's why I am so afraid of the idea that I will no longer be able to visit the mountains in particular or nature in general, along with the more existential anxiety that one day the mountains will still be there but my senses will be unable to take them in. Yet, as I've said, it's no small consolation to know that others will be able to do so. The knowledge of that, or at least the belief in it, is akin to E. O. Wilson describing the wolverine's existence, even though he himself never got to see it: the knowledge that something exists and will continue to do so.

The weather must be the reason why these thoughts surface the moment I reach the cabin this time—the absence of sun and the absence of color. There are days like this that are quite simply lifeless. It's early in the day and early in December, and a scant layer of pitiful white snow lies over the colorless terrain. The weather is mild and the lead-heavy cloud cover hangs over landscape and mind like a wet woolen blanket. I really have to get outside, so after firing up the stove, I wrap up warm, put on my boots, and head into the ridges south of the cabin. The mountains are stone dead and I can't shake off a kind of gloom that's dogged me for days now. A hint of sun would have done the trick, yes, even a tiny break in the clouds that might have revealed a glimpse of something brighter would have helped, but it is massively gray; wet cotton wool everywhere, even though the meager layer of snow on the ground is doing its best to lighten things up a bit. It really is a black-and-white world, like a photograph from my childhood. There's also just too much snow for walking to be especially pleasant; in some places, it conceals holes, in others, roots and rocks. In one place I see the parallel tracks of a mouse vanish into a hole in the snow beside a juniper bush. And that's it. The once omnipresent thrushes have left the mountains now. Until recently, they swooped around in noisy flocks living high on fall berries, but since the last snowfall they've sought out lower pastures. Most other birds have also abandoned the mountains; a raven, a flock of willow tits, and a few goldcrests are all I see. The tiny goldcrests offer a brief flash of color with their beautiful greenish-yellow backs and bright orange skullcaps.

On this particular day, I was planning to hike to Skarfjell and since everything in the forest is wet, I take the easiest and most open route across the bogs. From Skarfjell, I can see neither the nearby mountains to the east nor the big mountains to the north, toward Rondane and Jotunheimen. Everywhere, my eyes meet a gray blanket of fog. I find the tracks of a solitary ptarmigan, which has spent the night up here in a snow hollow before breakfasting on birch buds. Then it took wing, leaving a clear impression of its flight feathers in the wet snow. Already by three, twilight is falling and I walk back to the cabin, light the stove, and make a hearty stew of shredded reindeer meat with a sauce of local lingonberries that I picked right outside the cabin in August. For dessert, I stuff myself with last year's cloudberries, nothing but cloudberries and cream, as much as I can eat. Right now, it would actually be nice to have company here, but I pour myself a glass of cognac instead, replacing the bottle in the corner cabinet, where it can remain until any deserving souls turn up here. Me or some of the kids. Then I take out a book, this time Jon Krakauer's *Into the Wild*.

I'VE READ A LOT of books over my life, many of them in my youth. Back then, I read everything I could lay my hands on, from banal heroic epics to Dostoevsky. There's a handful I've reread three times, just to see if they still hold the same strong appeal I recall from the first reading—and they do. Two of the first books that left this kind of enduring impression were Helge Ingstad's *Land of Feast and Famine* and Fridtjof Nansen's account of the voyage of the *Fram* to the North Pole. It wasn't an especially original choice of literature; many boys my age read these books, which shaped their dreams. It is a masculine dream, this, to conquer the wilderness. To live out there from hunting and fishing, a taciturn life cut to the bone, balanced on the very brink of the abyss of existence. Although this, too, is natural romanticism, it's a different brand from Thoreau's wanderings and observations in a benign natural world where more time is devoted to cultivating herbs than fishing, and where hunting doesn't even feature. Part of the point is being *knowledgeable* about nature, familiarizing yourself with the movements and mentality of game animals, maintaining control for as long as possible in a marginal environment where you are at the mercy of the wilderness in every conceivable way. Mastering such a life is the ultimate test of masculinity. Canada, Alaska, and Kamchatka were places where a man could take his knife, fishing rod, and rifle and vanish into the wilderness. But the premise all the way was to know what awaited you, to understand and master nature, to have control. That's why I initially feel a certain irritation about the project Krakauer describes, a romantic and hopelessly ignorant city boy's wanderings in the heart of Alaska, where he ends his days by Mount McKinley. Motivation is the interesting factor here, his intense longing to be at one with nature; but there's more to it than that. His project is also a farewell to the lack of spiritual depth he has experienced in the consumer society, a search for something pure, uncompromising, and meaningful.

The book is based on the true story of a young man, Christopher McCandless, who burns all his bridges in 1992, hitchhikes to Alaska, and vanishes into the wilderness with a small-caliber rifle and a ten-pound sack of rice, apparently without any idea what he has let himself in for. It is a tale of obsession, yet something familiar still lies beneath it, and perhaps McCandless's obsession is a distillation of the desire to be at one with nature. Despite warnings from people familiar with the terrain, he first wanders around other inhospitable parts of the U.S. wilderness before setting off along the Stampede Trail in rotten spring snow in a state akin to religious obsession. In spring 1993 he was found in, of all places, an abandoned bus wreck in the deep and almost impenetrable forests where the Stampede Trail used to run before it became overgrown, dammed by beavers, and broken up by rain and rockfalls. He was found by moose hunters, and everything indicated that he had simply starved to death. But he had probably also been weakened by eating poisonous plants, likely in an attempt to live a vegetarian life, feeding off nature's bounty. And although Krakauer's disentangling of the factors that sent McCandless off on this fatal one-man expedition reveals him to have been an unusual, intelligent, introverted, and inquisitive boy, the most important inspirations for his expedition came primarily from literature: Jack London and Henry David Thoreau.

Among the items found alongside the emaciated remains of McCandless were a copy of *Walden*, with certain passages underlined, including this one:

> No man ever followed his genius till it misled him. Though the result were bodily weakness, yet perhaps no one can say that the consequences were to be regretted, for these were a life in conformity to higher principles. If the day and the night are such that you greet them with joy, and life emits a fragrance like flowers and sweet-scented herbs, is more elastic, more starry, more immortal—that is your success. All nature is your congratulation, and you have cause momentarily to bless yourself... The true harvest of my daily life is somewhat as intangible and indescribable as the tints of morning or evening. It is a little star-dust caught, a segment of the rainbow which I have clutched.[39]

Underlying this somewhat overwrought poetry is the will to use hunger and self-denial as the route to freedom; inspired by Thoreau, McCandless gives away all his worldly goods and symbolically burns his last banknotes before setting off into the wilderness for good. He, like Thoreau, also forsakes love. As Krakauer laconically notes:

> Like not a few of those seduced by the wild, McCandless seems to have been driven by a variety of lust that supplanted sexual desire. His yearning, in a sense, was too powerful to be quenched by human contact.

> McCandless may have been tempted by the succor offered by women, but it paled beside the prospect of rough congress with nature, with the cosmos itself.[40]

This pietistic and downright life-denying urge to be at one with nature is quite different from the rugged realism described by Jack London and Helge Ingstad, and is, at its deepest, a quest for meaning. Another of the passages McCandless underlines is from Boris Pasternak's *Doctor Zhivago*: "At such a time you felt the need of committing yourself to something absolute—life or truth or beauty—of being ruled by it in place of the man-made rules that had been discarded. You needed to surrender to some such ultimate purpose more fully."[41] Self-denial and the rejection of worldliness achieved by way of nature rather than the monastery, then—not that this is anything new. Since the dawn of time, wise men of all stripes have sought insight and meaning through a combination of asceticism, solitude, and nature.

In my youth, I would have devoured this story, but I think even then, I would have been alienated by the romanticism, the denial of life, the downright unnaturalness of it all. After all, the very essence of life, indeed everything that plays out in nature, is about reproduction, lust, and desire. I too am capable of purely erotic feelings in and about nature, but that serves as a complement to the biological, carnal lusts. McCandless is largely interesting as a representative of the ancient desire to find meaning through asceticism and a kind of merging with nature. But hunger and cold for the sake of suffering, as a penitentiary exercise, hold no appeal for me. Putting up with hunger and cold in the mountains is a different matter, but I am incapable of transcending myself and finding meaning in suffering as a goal in itself—with the exception of a hard slog. Slogging up a mountain can spark a very particular joy, not just when you finally reach the summit but along the way too. And I do believe in seeking both self-insight and also a kind of deeper insight into or oversight of existence through solitary time in nature. I am always at peace in nature, even, in some peculiar way, in difficult situations—on cliffs or in bad weather. Nature never means me any harm, but it's also foolish to think that it will extend me any concern. What it does offer, however, is this distance, especially from the day-to-day struggle to earn a crust down there among the teeming masses. A struggle that is difficult to entirely opt out of but which it is healthy to observe from the outside and from above now and then. Yes, we should be serious, but we should also take care not to set too much store by small and really meaningless things. There is much in life we would benefit from viewing with ironic distance, a certain devil-may-care attitude of the kind I imagine the wolverine may have.

What's more, there is no spiritual insight to be had from listening to "Mother Earth," as if nature had some profound, collective wisdom. Nature is not a clearly defined unit, and I feel no compulsion to merge with it, because how is that even possible? Nature has no shared consciousness or intent; it is—to the extent that we can even apply such a common description—a kind of collective replete with conflicts of interests, but at the same time an interwoven community of mutual interdependence. The trees and what we call the animals—the great, charismatic species, in other words, like wolverines and reindeer—are only fragments of a nature that is largely invisible, microscopic, and, to some extent, unknown. In a vaguely bounded part of nature that we can call the ecosystem, these actors all appear on the same stage, but it is a play with no director. Everyone is performing their own play, often at odds with others but overwhelmingly alongside them. Nature is just as much an arena of collaboration and symbiosis as it is "red in tooth and claw." It has no will or intrinsic harmony, but we can easily project our own sense of harmony upon it, and we gain a sense of belonging from thinking that here, too, I am one among many species—like the wolverine.

As the fire in the stove sinks from flames to embers I set aside *Into the Wild* with mixed feelings: a somewhat reluctant admiration for McCandless's idealistic refusal to compromise and irritation over the hopelessly romantic nature of his project. Although it's still fairly early in the evening, it's totally dark outside. No stars, no moon, no light anywhere, just a glimmer from the wet snow. Absolute silence reigns and I feel truly alone. Does the world still exist out there? I have big plans for the next day. Snow is forecast tonight, along with cooler temperatures, and sun tomorrow, and then more snow again toward evening. I'm looking forward intensely to sun on snow; it will be such a different experience from today. And I'm also looking forward to skiing, which is so different from wading into the mountains on foot. This time, I'll take a fair amount of equipment with me and spend a couple of nights in the mountains: one at Kluftbua and one at Borkebua. And I'm going to get a lot done. If there *is* a wolverine here in the mountains, I'm going to find it.

THE NEXT DAY, I wake early, full of anticipation about the day ahead and my ski trip. It's only six-thirty and still dark outside, but I can't sleep any more. So I take out the cabin's old visitors' book and read about previous trips into the mountains. I've written a lot of the entries in an unpracticed hand that still bears signs of the cursive lettering we were forced to learn in primary school. Generally speaking, they are descriptions of how many ptarmigans we've seen, a black grouse here, a fox's tracks there, which peaks we climbed, along with weather and conditions. Most of it is written in telegraphic style, with an occasional, cautious superlative if we'd seen more ptarmigans than usual, or if the weather and conditions had been especially good. The summer visits were fewer, but here too there are notes about fishing in the local lakes and rivers, cloudberry-picking trips and visits to the Breitjønn tarns—complete with enthusiastic descriptions of the northern phalarope. Eventually there are accounts of hunting trips too. We acquired an English setter, which was never much of a hunting hound; it never learned to point properly, although it managed to scare up plenty of ptarmigan broods before we got within shooting distance. It strikes me again how little I remember of these special experiences, although reading these entries does evoke them—it's like putting a negative in a bath of silver nitrate, the way we once did to develop our black-and-white photographs. Then I find the description of the first time I found the rough-legged buzzards' nest occupied—here, I've allowed myself a *fabulous!* I also describe the struggle with the bird box and my enthusiasm when goosanders nested there the following year. I treated myself to a *fabulous!* there too. This word, one I still use often when a description of experiences in nature needs a bit more oomph, has clearly been part of my vocabulary for a long time.

On my way up to the cabin, I stopped off at Mum's in Lillehammer to pick up three of my earliest *Nature Notes* from my boyhood room. The *Zoo Journal* and the books that followed, which I gave the slightly less pretentious name of *Nature Notes*, detailed all my notable experiences in nature. The big apple orchard and fields of strawberries that once lay on our neighbor's land beside my childhood home have been replaced with three huge square quad houses, and some years before that our local wood was built over; the meadows where the cows used to graze in summer and where we built our ski jump in winter met the same fate. We spent evening after evening in the cold winters building ever more daring jumps and setting ever more spectacular records. We didn't have much else to do with ourselves in that pre-digital age, but no one misses opportunities that don't exist. How radically changed everything is now, not just the landscape, but life and childhood. In my boyhood room there's a photo of my class on the first day of school. I stand there staring into the camera with a determined expression on my face: this was a solemn moment. At that point, I hadn't the faintest idea what my life would bring, and hadn't given it that much thought either. Now I know how it turned out and have good reason to be satisfied.

It's difficult to see any resemblance between myself today and the fair-haired lad in the picture. Only when I read my nature notes do I recognize ideas and values that must have been there from early on. These notes are more comprehensive than the ones in the visitors' book at the cabin, but still decidedly matter-of-fact. The Easter vacation from March 25 to April 1, 1972, detailed on the page after my first description of the wolverine tracks, is described as follows: "Heard black grouse courting several mornings outside the cabin (seven to eight in the morning). Spotted two black grouse and six ptarmigans during the vacation." The following year, under the heading "Double Luck," I've devoted an entire page to the first day of the Easter vacation. On our way up to the cabin, we stopped by a bird box that had been hung up the year before, where I experienced "a high point in my ornithological career." The box was occupied by a boreal owl and contained "three white owl eggs and a dead mouse." As if that wasn't enough, a moose appeared by the roadside shortly afterward and allowed us to contemplate it at close quarters for a good long time before vanishing into the forest. A great day. May 20, we are back at the cabin again and now there are six newly hatched chicks in the box, and fifteen mice arranged along the walls. I have sketched the entire scene. Yet even this event pales in comparison with June 2. That's the day we go off to hang up the famous large bird box made from a hollow log that we'd dragged in by sled the previous winter. It was hauled up and fastened to a branchy old spruce right beside the rough-legged buzzards' rock face, where it hangs to this day.

When we came out onto the bog under the sheer rock face where we knew there were a few old nests, a huge, majestic bird took off from a ledge on the cliff where the nest was located. I climbed up to it and there, on a bed of green spruce needles and feathers, lay four big rough-legged buzzard eggs, greenish yellow and speckled. A sensation and the high point of the summer.

I FOLLOW THIS UP with further visits later the same summer (no climbing up there those times): of the four fluffy chicks, two survive to become flight-ready youngsters. The first time I encountered the rough-legged buzzard here was April 29, 1972, when it suddenly swooped over my head near this cliff shrieking, and I "took two photos of the buzzard with my new 135mm telephoto lens." The doubtless blurred images are probably lying around in some box of old slides in Mum's attic, which is also full of unused memories and forgotten experiences.

Here, too, I see that my first hunting trip took place that same fall. On September 23, I go into the mountains with my Uncle Øyvind, although he's the only one with a rifle. He misses two hares, so I'm spared any blood and suffering, but the thrill of the hunt is still contagious. There will be many trips here with Dad in the years that follow. I also find the story of the time a moose cow with two calves chased me up a tree. The story as I've always told it is that I sat up the tree for a good long while, freezing to death, but it turns out that I had only just begun to clamber up the tree when the cow moved on. Memories are unreliable things, especially when competing with a good yarn that becomes more elaborate with every retelling. I can't claim to feel "as if it happened yesterday" when I relive these memories through my notes. Some events loom like mountain peaks over the sea of fog, but many of them merge to form diffuse, probably somewhat dubious recollections, and I'm not even sure whether they happened twenty or thirty years ago. Nonetheless, these episodes, along with all the others I've had throughout my life, represent cumulative life experience that isn't just the life itself but also an overview that comes with age and understanding of what is and isn't important.

And so these notes continue. Gradually other interests take over from the obsession with birds, although it is possible to tentatively combine them for a while. In 1977, I take my first girlfriend into the mountains from Breistølen. We camp out there overnight and she dutifully accompanies me to Inner Breitjønn tarn to record birds—a subject that is of zero interest to her. A bit later that summer, I record that it is "teeming with northern phalarope" at North Breitjønn tarn, where I also note the presence of a pair of ruffs, male and female, with a possible courtship ground, several pairs of velvet scoters, wood sandpipers, common redshanks, golden plovers, and common ringed plovers, as well as Lapland longspurs and fieldfares along the banks. There's a separate notebook called *Remarks and Notes: Birds and Bird Boxes*. It contains descriptions of times and places where I have found eggs and chicks in the bird boxes, breeding and hatching successes, as well as the eggs

I have seen, all with corresponding dates. I start the notes in 1966, the summer I was ten. The only thing I remember about that day was the uneasy thought that my age was now advancing from a single- to a double-digit number, and that I was highly unlikely to experience an age that ran to three digits. Even that early on, I felt that the countdown had started. My bird-watching activity peaks in 1972, when, aged fifteen, I record no fewer than twenty-six kinds of eggs, ranging from magpie on April 23 to common eider on July 5. Activity remains high for the next three years, but after that it eases off. Birds and nature were facing competition. I lie there late into the night leafing through these notes, which reflect the very essence of my teenage life. Here are notes about fishing trips with Dad, several of them during summer nights in which we explored unknown lakes and stretches of river. Most of these events I do not recall as specific memories, just separate highlights, yet they are still stored in a way and can be recalled in the form of images, emotions, and moods through these notes—or when I return to these specific places. I've had many such moments during my trips into the mountains. Here's where Dad hooked a huge trout with a fly, here's where I shot a ptarmigan which pretty much landed on top of us while we were resting behind a cliff on a mountain hike, there's the valley where we spent a bright summer night fishing our way up and down the river.

THE FOLLOWING DAY, I eat a hearty breakfast washed down with black coffee, pack some bread, a few pouches of freeze-dried food, matches, cheese, salami, jam, and a watertight bag of extra woolen clothes—two extra pairs of socks, extra mittens (I learned my lesson!), and a hat. As well as a sleeping bag. I've taken my map and compass and have dropped the GPS but am bringing along a few books and a proper headlamp. The evenings may be long. I put on a pair of sturdy water-repellent canvas pants and an anorak over the top of woolen underwear (there's a fleece jacket in my bag), as well as high gaiters, and backcountry ski boots. Then I lock the cabin behind me and follow the route I have so often taken before, toward Breistølen. It really did snow a lot last night, and it's still snowing lightly, but I see that there'll be sun in an hour or two.

The light pre-Christmas snow isn't properly packed over roots and rocks yet, so I opt for my old backcountry skis. However, yesterday's underlayer of wet snow has frozen, providing a perfectly decent base beneath the eight inches of fresh powdery snow from last night. As forecast, the sun comes out when I reach Breistølen. There's a reason for the sense of well-being triggered by light on snow: during the darkness of the Nordic winter, we used to be at chronic risk of vitamin D deficiency before the days of cod-liver oil and vitamin pills. Seeking out snow and sun in a light-poor winter may therefore be a highly rational choice, and the higher up you are in the mountains, the more light there is, especially ultraviolet light, which is particularly crucial for our skin's ability to synthesize vitamin D. In fact, the intense well-being we feel when the first rays of spring sunshine warm our skin is a signal that sun on skin isn't only harmful; and that Nordic tendency to tear off all our clothes and roast ourselves scarlet on the beach may have a similar explanation. The other rational reason for seeking out the glittering white plateaus is our need for melatonin, which plays an important role in sleep regulation, and whose production is induced by light. Light counteracts the sleep problems and depression of the darkest days. As far as I'm concerned, though, it's irrelevant whether the joy of sun on snow is as irrational as the beauty of a mountaintop, or the view we see from it. What matters is the effect, and I feel the same intense joy I experienced here in March, even though the sun back then bore the promise of spring, whereas this is a low and somewhat feeble winter sun. Still, after a dark and heavy November and early December, even this light gives me a tremendous kick.

As so many times before, I eat my packed lunch by a knoll southwest of Øverlihøgda, with the birch forest and the large boggy area, Stormyra, at my feet. Down there is where I spent the night in my hammock beneath a full moon. I've just startled a flock of a dozen or so ptarmigans farther down the mountainside, so it isn't totally dead here, and behind where I'm sitting, there are also ptarmigan tracks and wing marks in several places around the thicket. The raven is coping with the harsh winters here too. A couple fly overhead, uttering their metallic *korrp*, and peering down at regular intervals to see whether I might have any leftovers for them. If I had to guess, I'd say this was the pair that nest down by the river pool on the Breia. When I'm fully rested, I ski up to higher ground, into what is now virgin terrain. There are no people here midweek so early in

December, and only one hare has yet dared leave its tracks in the fresh snow, as it makes its way from its nighttime lair beneath a rock to its grazing grounds amid the brushwood and bushes along the Breia. Once, back when I still used to hunt up here, I shot a hare a bit farther into the mountains. It was a ghastly experience. I was skiing along in a slightly reverential state of mind, as now, when the hare suddenly dashed out in front of me at a decent distance. I was most inclined to let it go, but I was here for the hunting, after all . . . I shot it at slightly too close quarters, hit its hind leg, and got to hear the notorious death scream of this otherwise so silent animal. It took a while for me to work up to my next shot. I may have forgotten a lot about my specific experiences, but this one sits very deep—the limping hare whirling around, screaming. I can still summon up my feeling of distress, because the contrast between this scene and the pure, white, quiet landscape was so absolute. I wasn't in hunting mode, either, and had barely managed to switch on my hunter insensitivity. The death throes, the scream, the blood in the white snow.

The hare tasted good when I eventually ate it, but that was a totally unnecessary killing, just as ptarmigan hunting was. And even though shooting a ptarmigan is a different matter, it still takes a while to erase the impression of the terrified eyes of an injured bird. After a while, I ran out of good excuses for hunting. It feels good to pass this way and know that I can simply look forward to whatever I might happen to see, and I'm also spared the irritation of missing my target. Besides, as a hunter you inevitably develop a different relationship to nature.

You're there primarily as a hunter, so although you are by no means blind to the beauty, you experience the primal human's hunter pulse and you see nature with the hunter's gaze. In this mode, your awareness of the great within the small is lost.

Despite the low winter sun and the falling temperature, I almost get a springlike feeling as I ski along here, and yesterday's despondency is replaced with euphoria. The Breia is still open, but I see that there are animal tracks in the willow thickets along the river's edge, so I take a detour down into the river valley. Hares have been hopping all over the place here, maybe just one, maybe two or three different animals, but now they've found a spot to settle for the day. I also see parallel weasel tracks, and the occasional ptarmigan track, but no life. If you want to see animals in the mountains, dawn and twilight are the times to look, although the ptarmigans are obviously sitting here someplace or another. I also come across tracks on a totally different scale: a three-foot stride length and hoofprints. In the winter, I saw the tracks of a moose farther down toward Breistølen, and now it is taking the opportunity to graze on the willow thickets in the mountains before the snow arrives in earnest. And the size of the tracks tells me that this is an animal that has no need to seek cover in daylight—it'd be a match even for the wolverine or a pack of wolves. The moose has followed the riverbed on the other side for a while, casually waded across the river, and walked onward. It has walked here today and there are no return tracks, so the likelihood is that it's somewhere among the willow thickets a bit farther up the river valley.

Maybe around the next bend. A motionless moose can blend in with the forest, but here among the willow it will inevitably be highly visible, even though the thickets can sometimes tower almost six feet above the ground. I ski up onto the low ridge again and advance carefully, binoculars at the ready. Knowing that there's an overwhelming probability that a big moose is standing somewhere ahead of me sets my hunter's pulse racing. It reminds me of why I used to hunt once upon a time: it was that sharpening of the senses, the extra dimension of excitement. Yet at the same time, it shut out other impressions, because I was focusing on tracks and movements. At regular intervals, I go carefully out to the edge, seeking cover behind rocks or outcrops where possible, and scour the river valley with my binoculars.

The tracks continue. Down from the left runs a creek surrounded by tall willows and small birches. I can follow the tracks in here but cannot see that they continue up along the valley after this point. The animal is in here somewhere and has managed to find the one place where it is, in fact, invisible. My pulse quickens as I approach the stand of trees. I scan the creek bed with my binoculars but see no sign that it has turned off up that way either. When I am only fifty or sixty yards away, we spot each other simultaneously. It lifts its head with those great antlers above the willow thicket and looks in my direction. It's a large ox, with the large ox's self-assurance. We stand there for a while, the pair of us, sizing each other up, then it slowly turns and, like the unflappable colossus it is, strides away through the thicket the same way it came up. That's what

I call a dignified retreat. I've had many close encounters with moose and have developed considerable respect for them over the years. A couple of times, I've had to take to my heels, and until recently, I was even convinced that I'd spent a cold half hour up a tree after a chance encounter with a cow and two grown calves. In fact, I simply hid behind a tree, but that didn't feel dramatic enough in the telling. However, this ox has nothing to prove to me. The hunting season is over, and so is mating season. I'm just a minor irritant—but you can't be too careful with humans.

I ski onward and upward toward Breitjønn but quickly realize I'm going to have to keep away from marshes and willow thickets. The frost has not settled in the soil, whereas the wet snow has already formed a layer of ice on the ground farther up, which will be a nuisance for the reindeer. It isn't ideal for skis either. There's a belt of snow-covered grassy hills between the coarse talus slopes higher up, and there aren't yet enough skiable stretches of frozen bog farther down. When I reach the talus, I leave my skis behind and head to the top of Gråhøgda on foot. When I'm nearly at the cairn, I come across more ptarmigan tracks—rock ptarmigans this time. Following them with my binoculars I spy two birds tripping up toward the cairn. One hops up onto a rock. I've always felt great sympathy and admiration for these birds for the mere fact that they manage to survive the winter up here amid the snow and rocks, enduring week after week of bitter wind and cold on a starvation diet of buds from small plants. And now all the berries are snowed under too. And all the while, they themselves are on the menu of every single carnivore in the mountains, from weasels to falcons, rough-legged buzzards, foxes, and wolverines. What's more, from September until snowfall, they are pursued across the terrain time and time again by hunters and their hounds. Out of sheer respect for the ptarmigans I decide against hiking all the way to the top, withdrawing downhill instead, where I sit a while with my binoculars. There are no reindeer tracks to be seen, but tomorrow I'll go to Storkvien and scout its southern flank, down toward the remote valley of Samdalen.

The sun is already sinking, so I descend to Borkebua and settle in for a long evening. I've brought two books with me. At the cabin, I found a copy of Robert Pirsig's old classic, *Zen and the Art of Motorcycle Maintenance*. There are copious marks in the margin, and I recall that it made a big impression on me. Thoreau also got to come along again. It's cold in this stone cabin, so cold that my breath is visible. I send a grateful thought to the people who drove the firewood out here, and soon the little stove is giving off plenty of heat. The advantage of this cabin is that it is small and low-ceilinged, so you can bring the temperature up to bearable levels, roughly 50°F or 10°C, in just a couple of hours. I lie down in the upper bunk, where the temperature has crept up a few degrees, crawl into my sleeping bag, switch on my headlamp, and reread Pirsig.

He is also on a civilization-critical mission, and this, along with his reflections on proximity to nature, and the book's sprinkling of philosophy, is what appealed to my youthful self. Pirsig is on a motorbike trip with his ten-year-old son, traveling through the American landscape in the company of friends. Spectacular mountain passes, Montana, Yellowstone. He describes nature with absorption—pine forests and sunrises—but sees it all from the saddle of a motorbike. Now as then, I'm skeptical. The motorcycle may be a good metaphor for freedom, but when you're taking everything in from a noisy, gas-guzzling vehicle, it's hardly going to allow you to become truly absorbed in nature. However, his observations about the extent to which our experience of nature and life are objective, his critique of elements of scientific reductionism (not as a method, but as a factor that places limits on an open mind), and, here too, the way the anthill society trivializes how we reflect on the purpose of life—all these are familiar themes.

Of course, Pirsig has read his Thoreau. One evening as he and his son lie in sleeping bags in their tent and listen to the rain pounding the canvas and the thunder rolling in the mountains, he digs out a paperback copy of *Walden*. He wants to pass on his fascination for Thoreau to his son.

> After a while, I reach into my pack for the paperback by Thoreau, find it and have to strain a little to read it to Chris in the gray rainy light. I guess I've explained that we've done this with other books in the past, advanced books that he wouldn't normally understand. What happens is I read a sentence, he comes up with a long series of questions about it and then, when he's satisfied, I read the next sentence. We do this with Thoreau for a while, but after half an hour I see to my surprise and disappointment that Thoreau isn't coming through. Chris is restless and so am I. The language

> structure is wrong for the mountain forest we're in. At least that's my feeling. The book seems tame and cloistered, something I'd never have thought of Thoreau, but there it is. He's talking to another situation, another time, just discovering the evils of technology rather than discovering the solution.[42]

Personally, I read Thoreau the opposite way: I've always thought that, despite the anachronism, despite how radically different the world was in 1854, it had already set out on the path of escalating growth. The cities were growing, the forests were shrinking, speed and the hunger for material goods were already a factor, and that is why a surprisingly large number of his reflections remain relevant today. The increasing distance from nature, together with speed and modernity, created the need for slow time in nature, and that didn't begin with Thoreau. There are many possible sources of inspiration for the concept of "the noble savage," and one influential origin dates back to a beautiful May day in 1732, when twenty-five-year-old Carl Linnaeus rode out of Uppsala, dispatched by the university to the wilderness of northern Sweden, to the territory of the Indigenous Sami, then known to Swedes as the Lapps. As well as taking an intense, sheerly erotic pleasure in nature, the young Linnaeus also has an idealized attachment to "the natural." Despite the harsh conditions in which "the Lapps" lived, Linnaeus takes a romantic view of them, as a harmonious people in harmony with nature, free of envy and tyrannical power structures. "O, lucky Lapp, who, hidden thus in the outermost corner of the world, lives well, happily, and innocently! You sleep here beneath your reindeer skin, free from all care, strife, and disputes, and have no notion what envy is."[43] Later, in his exhaustive and profoundly moralistic "dietary guidelines," he once again highlights the pure, natural, and uncorrupted character of the Lapps. Linnaeus's description of this idyllic state of nature also became an important inspiration for Rousseau's cultural critique, but it is only a century later that Thoreau follows through on this critique systematically and philosophically in a way that still resonates—although not with Pirsig then and there.

Next morning the cabin is as cold as only a stone building can be in winter. Meaning that it could be a lot colder: the temperature is still above freezing, but only just. I feel as if I'm done with tents in winter, but it's almost as much of an effort to crawl out of my sleeping bag in a cabin. I light the stove and take my cooking kit back to the bunk where, from the warm embrace of my sleeping bag, I make myself first coffee, then porridge, which I sprinkle with a handful of raisins. It has begun to cloud over, and soon there'll be snow. The days are short at this time of year, and it's still daybreak when I cross the shallow valley and ski up to Storkvien by way of its gentle eastern flank. It starts to snow, but I pass a river of reindeer tracks on my way up that still look pretty fresh. The herd has crossed here, heading south toward Samdalen, but I see no reason to follow the tracks and needlessly unsettle these truly wild animals. They have a harsh winter ahead of them and the last thing they need is a scare. Still, it's easy to follow their trail with my binoculars from the summit and observe the herd from a distance. It turned east before Samdalen and now stands on the outer edge of a large stretch of bog, where the deer can still easily dig their way down to food.

My plan is to do a circuit of Storkvien's eastern side, above the birch forest that offers a view down toward the lake, Imsdalsvann, so I ski down the hillside in the direction of Imsdalen valley. There, I follow the course of a creek, crossing it above a waterfall, and continue toward the foot of the mountain in the southeast. The snow is falling ever more heavily, and when the visibility decreases to just a few yards, I give up, turn, and follow the side of the hill back west. The weather is changeable, and when the snow eases off again, I aim for the wolverine talus. From where I am, it's pretty easy to locate. Just before I reach it, I see a track leading into the talus. Once again, the sight of the legendary creature's track engenders a sense of sheer unreality. The wolverine has approached from the north, walked over the bluff where the mountain sharply descends, then continued in a straight line to the lower edge of the talus. Here, it has veered back up again, walking inside between two large rocks. It was very clear about where it was going: wolverines use their dens, food stores, and daytime lairs for generations. I stand and stare in fascination at the prints leading into the hole, which are covered in so little snow that the creature must have arrived here pretty recently. The tracks are big enough to suggest that he's a male, the wolverine lying in there just a few yards away from me. Maybe no more than a single yard. Does he know I'm standing outside? Probably. Is he afraid, for all his fearlessness? Yes, almost certainly: he is well aware that his only true foe in the world is standing right outside. A few wolverine generations back, he might have been smoked out of his den and shot, and these days, he can be killed under the population management program, so he has good reason to be afraid. After a reverential moment, I follow the wolverine trail back the way it came. Although it isn't exactly the same as following a wolverine in the hope of catching a glimpse of it, I *am* still following it, only backward. Even if I didn't get to see it, I know what lies at the end of the trail: a wolverine in the talus. If I could follow this trail backward in time, it would eventually merge with the tracks of this wolverine's parents, and many generations of wolverines going all the way back to 1972 and the wolverine tracks my father and I found. There's probably a family connection between that wolverine and this one, possibly separated by as few as five generations, though more likely ten. At any rate, it is a fascinating idea that there's a continuous series of wolverine tracks going back not just fifty but thousands of years in time; a continuous chain of unbroken wolverine life, just as there is a continuous, unbroken chain of life that goes back 3.5 billion years in time. All from the same origin, everything related. Compared with almost all other life-forms, the wolverine and I are very closely related, and I sense this kinship as I follow the trail in the direction from which it came. It crosses the summit, then goes down the other side, straight toward Kluftbua. He stopped off in a willow thicket and, as Kluftbua comes into view, the trail veers upward toward Gråhøgda. I follow it with my binoculars and see that it comes from above the spot on the mountainside where I found the reindeer skeleton in June.

He probably helped himself to some of that earlier, and maybe he stopped by there just now, in the hope of finding some remnants of fibers or bone marrow. There can hardly have been anything left, not even for a wolverine. I follow the tracks farther upward toward the summit, but the snow grows heavier again, and dusk is approaching, accompanied by a pallid moon that is quickly dimmed by the snowfall. The temperature drops toward 5°F/-15°C, so I decide to take a break and return to the talus later.

I pole down to Borkebua, light the stove, and fix myself a pouch of freeze-dried chicken stew using hot water from my thermos. After eating, I fill the oven to the brim with coarse logs that will burn slowly, then put on my headlamp and follow my own, partly snow-covered ski tracks back to the wolverine talus. I stand at a slight distance, and circle around it until I meet my own trail, but see no tracks leading out.

Back at the cabin, I stand outside for a while. The snow has stopped, but the pale crescent moon still isn't shedding much light, and it is utterly silent. I'm probably a dozen miles from the nearest human being. Back inside, the cabin's getting nice and warm. There are some candles here, which I light, and then I take Thoreau out of my bag again. Even though Pirsig is right to say that his language is sometimes too rich in metaphor and florid, Thoreau still has a timeless appeal. There's a reason why you'll find lists of his best quotes, and why his desire to live life to the full, in thought and deed, will always and inevitably strike a chord with someone. A wish like that can be fulfilled in many ways, but Thoreau's way was to live *in* and *with* nature.

Understandably, he resonates with more people today than back in the days when the world still felt infinite and rich in promise, when material progress and the great acceleration had barely begun, and the skies were still clear. Turning away from this promise, from the future itself, and back toward the nature we had at last managed to escape and were in the process of conquering was, as Thoreau himself acknowledges, a niche interest. Still, the main point of living in nature was always to seek the essence of his own life and human life in general. Not by seeking any deeper wisdom from nature itself, for no such wisdom exists, but by seeking out what can be summed up as a rich life by simple means. "Our life is frittered away by detail. An honest man has hardly need to count more than his ten fingers, or in extreme cases he may add his ten toes, and lump the rest. Simplicity, simplicity, simplicity! I say, let your affairs be as two or three, and not a hundred or a thousand."[44]

Complexity breeds more complexity, haste breeds more haste, and endless demands for greater efficiency. Thoreau has made the railroad the object of his hatred, and it has now made inroads in the vicinity of Walden, transporting more people and more goods at ever-increasing speeds.

> It lives too fast. Men think that it is essential that the *Nation* ... talk through a telegraph, and ride thirty miles an hour ... If we do not get out sleepers, and forge rails, and devote days and nights to the work, but go to tinkering upon our *lives* to improve *them*, who will build railroads? And if railroads are not built, how shall we get to heaven in season?[45]

This was written one hundred and seventy years ago. My father was born just seventy years after *Walden* came out, and life in those days was not substantively different from life in 1854. The world was still in expansion, the forests extensive, the sky blue, there were unknown wildernesses, and nature was endless and invulnerable. In the course of Dad's life, everything took off: thirty miles an hour became a hundred and thirty, the telegraph became the internet, the world he left was busier and more efficient than the one he was born into. He came from an age where everything was scarce and left this world surrounded by excess. I realize that the pleasure I take in being able to spend the night alone here in a small spartan mountain cabin stems from the fact that everyday life is anything but spartan. I always have enough of everything—except time. I am always surrounded by people, I am never cold, never hungry. If I experience exhaustion and danger, it's because I have sought them out myself so that I can feel I am alive. I have lived in the world's best age but feel a profound unease about what now lies ahead. About the world my children and especially my grandchildren will live in. Humanity has probably always felt that it stands at an inflection point, but now we indisputably do, because we have reached some physical boundaries that force us to realize that the tree cannot grow into the sky indefinitely.

Thoreau doesn't answer the question of whether repetition will be enough to fill our lives or give it some kind of meaning. Mustn't we always have the goal of traveling onward, farther, higher, faster? Could we live well at thirty miles an hour today, or fifteen? With pen and ink? With slowness? Do we not need visions of a future that is different from today? Since Thoreau, indeed in the past fifty years alone, we have acquired a whole new assortment of professionalized distractions: Twenty-four-hour access to media-created celebrities in all kinds of reality shows. A continuous digital flood of diversions that eat up our time without attempting to offer so much as a veneer of meaning or significance. And all this occurs within the self-reinforcing cycle of the market's blind logic and endless growth in time-consuming distractions and entertainment. We have every opportunity to escape a challenging idea or a minute of dead time or solitude, and this too is a form of collective lobotomization. On top of all this, we are left with a feeling that life is running away from us uncontrollably, and a sense of stress and frustration at our inability to keep up with everything. Thoreau and Zapffe would have seen their nightmares realized. Growth is not an agreed policy even though it is the consequence of market logic. What's more, it is an intrinsic, competition-driven part of the system that is propelled by its own gravitational force. This development also appears to have an built-in ratchet system: it travels perfectly well in one direction but resists the reverse. Controlled degrowth seems, for now, to be a utopia.

The world has also moved on in other, more constructive ways: we live longer, are healthier, and have more opportunities for self-realization. More importantly, we have become more humane, norms have been supplemented by the ethics and rules a society must have, and we know more. Our knowledge of the world, from atom to cosmos, has also grown exponentially. The world is digitally connected, giving us access to endless information about everything. And, for better or for worse, we live our lives through our cell phones. The problem with this is the resultant information overload that challenges our ability to sort the wheat from the chaff, and gives us a justified sense of being at the mercy of the algorithms. But the world has changed, and there has always been a thrilling uncertainty about what lies around the next bend. Would we be able to bear it if the next bend were just part of a familiar circle that always returned to the well-trodden track? Perhaps, if we didn't know anything else, but having tasted the fruits of progress, it is impossible to turn back—until we *must*.

And since Thoreau argued for living a rich life by simple means, an additional reason has emerged for doing so. Or rather, the argument that nature is a source of that rich life remains unchanged, but it has simply become more relevant today because the traits of society that Thoreau warned against have all been exacerbated. What *is* new, however, is that this has now become an issue that affects the future of both the planet and generations as yet unborn. An approach that seemed totally irrelevant a hundred and seventy years ago, and which, even in 1972, was a topic discussed by a mere handful of future skeptics is no longer a possibility but a reality. We are living beyond our means, or at least beyond our sustainable means. In 2022, Earth Overshoot Day fell on July 28. That is the day of the year when, as far as we can calculate, we have consumed the planet's annual capacity. The rest of the year we live on credit—no, we steal from the people who will have to live here in fifty, five hundred, or fifty thousand years. If everyone in the world lived as extravagantly as we do in Scandinavia, Earth Overshoot Day would have fallen earlier, in April. Yet as recently as 1972, we were living in a close-to-sustainable society. Has life become better, happier, indeed more meaningful in the intervening years?

To mark the fortieth anniversary of the publication of *The Limits to Growth* in 2012, one of its authors, Jørgen Randers, wrote *2052*, a kind of prediction for the next forty years. He notes first that the most pessimistic forecasts from 1972 are the ones that have come to pass: the world has been too slow to react, CO_2 emissions and the loss of nature have continued, and no imminent solutions are in sight. On the positive side, he thinks that the global population will peak around 2040 at "just" 8.1 billion. This, combined with a weak economy, problems caused by climate change, and a depleted resource base, should make global consumption decrease faster than expected (and faster than is desirable for many people, of course). The world will become worse, but will still remain inhabitable until 2052, says Randers, with some reservations, of course. Well, we have already passed 8 billion and the one thing we know about the world fifty years from now is that it will be very different. And fifty years is just around the corner. There ought to be wolverine tracks here in the mountains in five thousand years' time too, reindeer for it to hunt, and people who can experience the joy and awareness of being alive. But if we continue on our current course, parts of the planet will become at least periodically uninhabitable by 2100, according to today's climate forecasts. The Amazon may be becoming savanna, the Great Barrier Reef will be dying, the Greenland ice will be melting irreversibly, and the permafrost thaw will pour more CO_2 into the atmosphere. The average global temperature could be close to three degrees higher than today, and much higher than that in certain places. Areas of the Arctic have already seen this kind of warming in the past forty years and, as ice cover in the north shrinks, the warming will escalate, thawing massive expanses of permafrost; there will be more forest fires, even in the north, and that will release large amounts of CO_2 into an atmosphere that already contains too much of it. Heat waves, droughts, and floods of biblical proportions will make life harder, while food production and access to clean water will dwindle. Large numbers of people will flee from areas that are periodically or permanently uninhabitable. Sea levels may be three feet higher than now—and rising; more of the world's ecosystems and species may have vanished forever. The world will still exist, we humans too, but shouldn't our ambitions for ourselves and our planet go beyond mere survival?

While a perfect future is not achievable, we *can* still avoid the grimmest scenarios. Warnings that our consumption, including our consumption of nature, was out of control came as early as 1972. And yet this was a dystopic subject reserved for experts and romantics. Growth was still a necessity while nature was a luxury that would always be in plentiful supply. Beyond all this, if we look fifty years back in time, that gives us a hint of how difficult it is to make predictions fifty years into the future. Our pleasures and pains, dreams and ambitions will likely be the same, but most other elements of our everyday lives today weren't even on the radar in 1972. Development is the deciding factor, and experience shows that development is an unpredictable beast, driven by its own dynamic. However, we must have some visions and wishes for where we want to go, what kind of goals we want for our society. What makes for a rich life, a good life, and, to the extent that it is possible, a meaningful life? And for anyone who thinks the reply to all that should be "more of everything," my answer is: that door must remain locked.

This outlook is also one of the reasons why I feel such a profound peace in this simple cabin. Life here is balanced in every way, in material terms too. Elsewhere in my life, I am plagued by chronic guilt because I, too, am plundering from the unborn, contributing to higher CO_2 emissions and the depletion of nature. I feel intense shame every time I travel by plane, and discomfort over the awareness that my daily life is eroding the world's resources. I simply do not do enough. Life in the cabin is sustainable, but a life like this is only possible over the long term if I opt out.

People always claim that shame and guilt don't solve any problems, but over the course of evolution, these feelings have arisen and survived because they have prompted us to treat our fellow humans better, motivating us to adopt behavior that would result in less shame and a clearer conscience. I certainly find that motivating. Until recently, I have been concerned about the future with only one hemisphere of my brain. I haven't felt any direct anxiety on behalf of my grandchildren and nature, and I still don't, but what I do now feel, with both hemispheres of my brain, is a profound unease. The world is facing something entirely new, and that is not good news. It's barely possible to picture this from a peaceful cabin deep in the mountains, surrounded by a darkness that feels safe, not menacing. And which feels very much as it did on my first night here many decades ago, only slightly more comfortable. The mountains are here, just as they were fifty years ago, and since, after all, the changes occur slowly and gradually compared with the speed of our lives, most of us find it difficult to take in the totality of the changes, so difficult as to border on the impossible. For those of us used to helping ourselves from the top shelf "because I'm worth it," because I feel like it, or because I can afford it—for us, our generation and our children's generation, sudden denial of that option will feel like a restriction on our freedom. And it is harder to adapt to a reversal in development than it was for my father to get used to a life that went from extreme frugality to the affluent society he experienced in his later years. But he wasn't entirely at ease with affluence either, because, deep down, he was driven by the imperative of frugality: work before pleasure, take only what you need, eat all the food on your plate, never throw anything away. For a while, I saw these as anachronistic attitudes, vestiges of a Western Norwegian pietism that was on its way out—until I realized that it was a kind of moral anchor. Besides, my father was a generous, life-loving man who had managed to shake off religion-based duty ethics.

So how do we adapt to the necessary reversal? This is where the small pleasures come in, pleasures and meaningful aspects of life that do not need reinventing. They are already at the top of the list of all the things that make life worth living: love, friends, nature, family, freedom—or days in the mountains spent searching for wolverine tracks. Freedom *from* rather than freedom *to*. We just have to make room for these pleasures, give them breathing space, but this can only happen via a kind of collective adaptation to a new situation. And that doesn't imply stagnation: when it comes to knowledge, insight, and wisdom, growth must certainly continue, ensuring that new knowledge awaits us around the next bend. I think a lot of us want to take this route, we just don't quite know how to break out of a model in which what used to be the goal has become the meaning. For my grandfather, the toil on his farm and in his fishing boat was motivated by material progress; he wanted to spare his children the same toil that had marked his own existence. That undoubtedly also gave meaning and direction to his life. For my father, this dream was achieved, but it didn't stop there. Development continued, driven by its own gravitational force, like a snowball in wet snow. Growth spawned more growth. There was never any point at which it was enough. We may well have reached this turning point now, compelled by the fact that we haven't just reached the limits but have far overshot them. That means we must not resist and yearn to return to a world in constant growth, but find out what makes life worthwhile in these new circumstances.

Anyone who spends a lot of time in nature grows to love nature and therefore also wishes for its continued existence. Many would claim that lost nature and climate change are caused by the absence of *spirituality*, by the triumph of materialism over faith. I am a nonbeliever, so I don't believe that. Or rather, I accept that the triumph of materialism is the problem, but religion has also been responsible for legitimizing the boundless liberties we have taken with nature and other species—and, historically speaking, it has hardly lacked an appetite for worldly goods. Faith can, at best, be an ally, but the alternative we need to counter a destructive materialism is considerably closer to hand and is far more concrete: nature itself. Nature, too, gives us the sense of something greater than ourselves, something different. "Nature is my cathedral" may be a cliché, but that's precisely because it resonates with so many people; it's a cathedral that doesn't demand incense and submission, commandments and prohibitions, but can instead offer us the freedom and clarity of thought to see what really matters. It doesn't require us to live a life of constant asceticism, only to spend sufficient time out there in nature to appreciate the rich life by simple means.

I TAKE OUT the last of the three nature journals I've brought with me. This one is called *Notes: Hikes—Nature*, and starts in March 1981, two months after my sister died:

> It's hard to find sources of enjoyment now that Marit is gone. Everything seems irrelevant, it's impossible to see any bright spots in everyday life. I hope and believe, that now as before, nature will have the most to offer me, and that is where I will find the greatest comfort. From now on, there will be less frantic exercising and more fine hikes in forests and mountains.

It continues with one such therapeutic hike early in March: I go off to climb Snøhetta, once believed to be the highest mountain in Norway, with two friends; after three days of snowstorms in the mountains I still conclude that it was "an enjoyable trip despite the disappointing weather. It did me good to get a spot of fresh air." And it did. Nature has always been there for me when times are hard, and, as I said earlier, life can never be totally empty as long as nature is there to be visited, like a silent psychotherapist. It demands nothing, it doesn't give any answers either, it simply *is*, but that's enough.

In a way, I feel that the circle is closed up here in the mountains. I believe this is the way I also thought when I was very young, as I can see from my school essays from the early 1970s, which are full of naive exhortations to care for nature and cause less pollution. My father also impressed on me that frugality was a virtue, not through his words but through his actions. These past fifty years may encompass my real life: everything that came before was a prelude; and although in many ways I feel the same now as I did then, I must, realistically, admit that I have now embarked on the postlude. In some peculiar way, life manages to be both long and short. A week goes by incredibly fast, and so does a year. And yet a year can contain so very much. And 1972 is just a hazy memory on the horizon, way back there. Another age, another life. As I leaf through these notes, I remember that Marit and I, or perhaps it was just me, had a feeling in fall 1980 that our parents' relationship could do with a boost. We bought a—for us—expensive pewter bowl, ornamented and decorated, and had it engraved with the message: "New light, new life, new hope. To Mum and Dad, from Marit and Dag. 12/31/1980." It was their wedding anniversary. Some days later, on a cold January night in 1981, Marit died without warning. So much for light, life, and hope. Had I been nice enough to my kind little sister? If only I had guessed what lay ahead—although who would actually want to know? After I blow out the last candles, the only light left is a reddish glow from the vent in the stove. Even though it's pitch-black outside and totally silent, it takes me a long time to get to sleep.

It's still dark when I get up the next morning, but dawn is on its way. I make the usual pot of black coffee, cut a few slices of bread, and shave off a few shreds of cured reindeer heart—salty, dark, and tasty. Then I get dressed, go out into the gray light of dawn, and do a round of the willow thicket that grows just above the cabin. This is where I had one of my greatest experiences of nature, maybe the greatest one ever, forty years ago. Ten years after I saw the tracks for the first time. That's the main reason why I chose precisely this spot as the hub of my search for wolverine tracks.

Two days before Christmas in 1978, I was up here ptarmigan hunting and spent the night in this little cabin. I had just finished the semester at the University of Oslo, had taken my exams, and was longing desperately for snow, skis, mountains, and freedom. Then as now, I'd skied on a thin layer of snow from my own cabin that morning, headed in through the birch forest and mountain, where ptarmigan tracks embroidered the snow around small bushes and heather-clad ridges. But ptarmigan flocks are shy at this time of year, and my reactions were poor with mittened hands and temperatures of -13°F/-25°C, so I came back to the cabin empty-handed. In the early evening gloom, with only a burned-down candle for light, it was just as well to creep into my sleeping bag—a light summer one, because, after all, I'd be sleeping indoors. The cabin was less comfortable back then. There wasn't so much as a stick of firewood, the temperature was the same inside as out, and the thin mattress on the narrow hard bunk gave only the illusion of a bed. My sleep became restless when the cold really started to bite through the sleeping bag at daybreak. I had to go out into the predawn twilight to try and warm up. Picking up my rifle, I staggered out and set off up to a field of willow thicket. And that's when it burst out like a black shadow. For a single frozen moment, we stood just feet apart, then it bared its teeth, spun around, sauntered up toward Gråhøgda until it was only a dark dot at the end of the trail, and vanished at last over the edge. In the seconds that followed, pulse racing, I was filled with a sensation I still cannot name. Happiness, gratitude, elation. Overwhelmed by what I had just experienced, I continued my circuit around the cabin and, as if to crown the moment, the sun sent its first rays over the ridge and revealed a reindeer flock a little higher up the mountainside over which the wolverine kept watch. I am incapable of offering a truly worthy description of this, my first and only encounter with a wolverine. Just as I can barely explain what made it such a glorious experience. But there was something unique about meeting it eye to eye, both of us equally surprised—and quite different from seeing it walk away, like a dancing black dot at the end of a trail that stretched out into the plateaus. I remember I caught myself thinking that it was a good thing I'd had my rifle with me in case it had attacked, a possibility I didn't consider unthinkable back then, and yet I felt no fear as I stood there. The only thing I felt was gratitude.

In the dawn light beside that same willow thicket forty years later, I can still summon up that sensation. In another forty or fifty years, much will be changed, but the mountain will remain, at least, and I am pretty certain that the wolverine will be here, the reindeer too. I myself will not, but this thought gives me peace: some things *will* be the same.

I continue calmly up to the wolverine talus one last time. Light snow fell last night and once again, I circle around the talus, as I did yesterday. No tracks lead out of it and the tracks leading in are barely visible now, as if the animal inside never existed. The hunt stops here.

"I have never seen a wolverine," writes the evolutionary biologist E. O. Wilson, "and I hope I never will." That seems like a paradoxical statement from a passionate nature lover who would surely be capable of appreciating a glimpse of the legendary animal, but it makes sense to me. Wilson explains it in these beautiful terms in *The Creation*:

> Its savage demeanor is not, however, why I want to avoid the wolverine. The reason is that I find *Gulo gulo* the embodiment of wildness, and I know there will still be untrammeled habitats on Earth if wolverines still roam there. I trust they will hold on in the vast subarctic forest, somewhere in North America or

> Eurasia, in places too far to be reached easily by vehicles or shank's mare. Wildlife biologists will need to know the general status of the wolverine in order to save the species, but I hope there always will be remote sections of its range barred to trappers and even scientists. Please let part of the wolverine stay a mystery![46]

"Everything is not created for the human gaze," writes author Erlend Loe in his enthusiastic review of the documentary *The Snow Leopard*, which brings out precisely this point: the almost mythological nature of a predator that survives in tiny numbers in places where humans really have no business being. Even though the wolverine is overseen and regulated, so thoroughly *managed*, a vestige of the mythical and the mystical still hangs over it.

For most of our prehistory, we were a handful of people in an endless wilderness, at the mercy not just of wind and weather but wild animals too. Because we have now tamed the wilderness, subjugated nature, and cushioned our existence with all the things modern society has to offer, life has become safer, simpler, and longer, but perhaps also a little bit too safe? That is why the remnant of wilderness and wildness that the wolverine represents is also a glimpse of something that has been lost and that, perhaps, we miss deep down.

BACK AT THE CABIN, I roll up my sleeping bag, swallow a last mouthful of cold coffee, and pack my bag. I run my eyes over the room one last time to make sure I haven't forgotten anything, take one last glance through the window that faces in the direction of the wolverine talus. Then

I lock the door, put on my skis, and set off. The snow is back in full force. Not hard, lashing grains this time, but big snowflakes. They feel nice and cool against my face. I stick out my tongue and taste them, the way we did as children. Soon it is snowing so heavily that visibility is poor, so once again I follow the safe river valley down toward the west. Behind me, my ski tracks are erased. In a few hours, no one will be able to see that anyone ever passed this way.

Acknowledgments

IT FEELS NATURAL to start off by thanking Dad: this started with him. He was the one who took me out into nature, and it was with him that I first discovered the wolverine tracks. You were an exemplary father. As always, I owe my editor, Erik Møller Solheim, a big thank you. Perhaps bigger than usual, because *Wolverine Tracks* involves many tracks that must intersect and interweave, and this book is very different from anything I've written before. Your sharp eye for what belonged where, for repetition, and for unnecessary distractions was crucial. I also wish to thank Eivind Faldet and Espen Rusten of the Norwegian Nature Inspectorate for a fabulous day out in the realm of the wolverine, for sharing their extensive knowledge about the animal, and for really setting me on its trail. In this English edition, I would like to thank my translator Lucy Moffatt for her careful and elegant translation. My thanks also to the many people who shared their stories about and meetings with wolverines, as well as books about the animal—far too many to mention here without the risk of leaving someone out. As we say in Norway: None named, none forgotten!

Translator's Note

For reasons of readability, the Norwegian titles of all books the author quotes in the body of the book have been translated, even where no English translation of the text is available. The original Norwegian title is cited along with the translated title in the notes.

Unless otherwise specified, all quotations from Norwegian books or poems were translated by Lucy Moffatt.

Notes

1 E. O. Wilson, *The Creation: An Appeal to Save Life on Earth* (New York: W. W. Norton & Company, 2006), 55–57.

2 Mikkjel Fønhus, *Jerv* [Wolverine] (Oslo: Aschehoug, 1959), 21–22.

3 Fønhus, *Jerv*, 18.

4 Fønhus, *Jerv*, 59.

5 Fønhus, *Jerv*, 81.

6 Jon Michelet, *Jerv* [Wolverine] (Oslo: Aschehoug, 1983).

7 Henry David Thoreau, *Walden; or, Life in the Woods* (Boston: Ticknor and Fields, 1854), 98.

8 Thoreau, *Walden*, 45.

9 Thoreau, *Walden*, 143.

10 Estwick Evans, *A Pedestrious Tour, of Four Thousand Miles, Through the Western States and Territories, During the Winter and Spring of 1818* (Concord, NH: Joseph C. Spear, 1819), 6.

11 Christopher Hansteen, *Reise-erindringer* [Recollections of travel] (Christiania [Oslo]: Christian Tønsbergs Forlag, 1859), 35.

12 Theodor Caspari, *Norsk naturfølelse i den nittende aarhundre* [The Norwegian feeling for nature in the nineteenth century] (Christiania [Oslo]: Aschehoug, 1917), 20.

13 Fridtjof Nansen, *Nansens røst Bind II* [Nansen's voice, vol. II] (Oslo: Dybwads Forlag, 1942), 577–78.

14 Fridtjof Nansen, *Friluftsliv: blad av dagboka* [Outdoor life: Pages from the journal] (Oslo: Dybwads Forlag, 1940), 88.

15 Nansen, *Nansens røst Bind II*, 220. Transcript of a speech delivered to the Norwegian Trekking Association in 1921.

16 Fridtjof Nansen, *Idrætsboken Bind I* [The sports book, vol. I] (Christiania [Oslo]: Aschehoug, 1922), foreword.

17 Henry David Thoreau, "A Winter Walk," in *Excursions* (Boston: Ticknor and Fields, 1863), 113–19.

18 Robert Collett, *Norges pattedyr* [Norway's mammals] (Christiania [Oslo]: Aschehoug, 1911–12), 362.

19 Michael W. Fox, *Concepts in Ethology: Animal and Human Behavior* (Minneapolis: University of Minnesota Press, 1974), 9.

20 Henry David Thoreau, *Early Spring in Massachusetts* (Cambridge, MA: The Riverside Press, 1883), 215–16.

21 Egil Hyldmo, *Jervboka* [The wolverine book] (Melhus, Norway: Snøfugl Forlag, 2000), 58.

22 John Vaillant, *The Tiger: A True Story of Vengeance and Survival* (New York: Vintage Books, 2011), 25.

23 Henry David Thoreau, "Walking," in *Excursions*, 161.

24 Thoreau, "Walking," 164–65.

25 Thoreau, "Walking," 188–89.

26 Rebecca Watters, "Return of the Wolverines," *The Wolverine Blog*, March 11, 2022, egulo.wordpress.com/2022/03.

27 Douglas H. Chadwick, *The Wolverine Way* (Ventura, CA: Patagonia Books, 2010), 181.

28 Chadwick, *The Wolverine Way*, 130.

29 Thoreau, *Walden*, 8.

30 Peter Wessel Zapffe, "Fjeldet i fare" [The mountain in danger], in *Kulturelt nødverge* [Cultural self-defense] (Oslo: Pax Forlag, 1997), 59.

31 Peter Wessel Zapffe, *Hvordan jeg blev så flink og andre tekster* [How I got so clever and other writings] (Oslo: Aventura, 1986), 106.

32 Thoreau, *Walden*, 41, 10.

33 Thoreau, *Walden*, 152.

34 Peder W. Cappelen, *Alene med vidda* [Alone with the plateau] (Oslo: Gyldendal Norsk Forlag, 1964).

35 Kerstin Ekman, *Løpe ulv* [The wolf run] (Oslo: Aschehoug, 2022).

36 Bergljot Børresen, *Den ensomme apen* [The solitary ape] (Oslo: Gyldendal Norsk Forlag, 1996).

37 Jens Andreas Friis, *Tilfjelds i Ferierne, eller Jæger- og Fiskerliv i Høifjeldene* [Into the mountains in the vacations, or hunting and angling life in the highlands] (Copenhagen: Gyldendal, 1910), 2–4.

38 Thoreau, *Walden*, 142.

39 Thoreau, *Walden*, 233.

40 Jon Krakauer, *Into the Wild* (London: Pan Macmillan, 2011), 67.

41 Krakauer, *Into the Wild*, 188.

42 Robert M. Pirsig, *Zen and the Art of Motorcycle Maintenance* (New York: William Morrow and Company, 1974).

43 Carl Linnaeus, *Flora Lapponica* (Stockholm: Kungl. Svenska Vetenskapsakademien, 1905), 229.

44 Thoreau, *Walden*, 99.

45 Thoreau, *Walden*, 100.

46 Wilson, *The Creation*, 57.